This Time is Different

H.K. Marwood

Published by Fireside Books, 2025.

AF721770

While every precaution has been taken in the preparation of this book, the publisher assumes no responsibility for errors or omissions, or for damages resulting from the use of the information contained herein.

THIS TIME IS DIFFERENT

First edition. November 8, 2025.

Copyright © 2025 H.K. Marwood.

ISBN: 979-8232790264

Written by H.K. Marwood.

Chapter 1: A Strange Stillness in the Air

There is a particular quality to the air before a storm breaks—a heaviness, a strange luminosity to ordinary objects, a pressure that makes dogs restless and birds fall silent. The meteorologists call it a pressure system; our ancestors simply called it weather-sense, that knowledge in your bones that something is coming.

Markets have their own atmospheric conditions.

In the spring of 1637, in the taverns and coffeehouses of Amsterdam, a peculiar calm had settled over the city. For nearly three years, the Dutch Republic had been seized by what we now call Tulip Mania—the world's first documented speculative bubble. Tulip bulbs, particularly the rare striped varieties affected by a mosaic virus, had become more valuable than houses. Ordinary citizens—weavers, blacksmiths, bakers—had abandoned their trades to become tulip traders. Fortunes were made overnight.

But by February, something had changed. The auctions continued, contracts still exchanged hands, yet a certain hesitation had entered the market. People still spoke of endless profits, but their voices carried a forced confidence. Tavern debates about bulb prices grew more strident, as though volume could substitute for conviction.

No one wanted to be the first to say it: the air had changed.

When the collapse finally came, it arrived not with a dramatic crash but with a simple absence—buyers who had promised to appear simply didn't. A planned bulb auction in Haarlem found its hall half-empty. Contracts went unfulfilled. Within weeks, bulbs that had traded for thousands of guilders couldn't be sold for hundreds.

The aftermath was not universal ruin as popular history sometimes suggests—the Dutch economy absorbed the shock—but something more subtle happened: a collective recalibration of reality. What had seemed entirely reasonable in January appeared plainly absurd by March.

This pattern—this strange stillness before economic realignment—repeats with remarkable consistency across centuries and cultures.

Consider October 1929. The American economy had soared through the Roaring Twenties on credit, confidence, and new technologies like radio and automobiles. The stock market had climbed so consistently that many believed a "permanent plateau of prosperity" had been achieved. Financial experts assured the public that stocks were fairly valued, that the fundamentals were sound.

Yet in the weeks before Black Thursday, something shifted. Trading volume thinned. Market veterans reported an indefinable tension on the exchange floor. Newspaper financial sections maintained their optimism, but with a brittle quality, as though the writers were trying to convince themselves as much as their readers.

The air had changed.

What makes these moments so difficult to navigate is that they contain no obvious alarm bells. The economic indicators often remain positive. Official statements project confidence. Those who express concern are dismissed as pessimists or fear-mongers.

In September 2007, Federal Reserve Chairman Ben Bernanke assured Congress that the subprime mortgage crisis would likely not spread to the broader economy. The stock market hit new highs that October. By December, the United States was entering what would become the Great Recession.

These periods of strange stillness share common psychological features. There is what economists call "preference falsification"—people publicly expressing confidence while privately harboring doubts. There is "herding behavior," where individuals suppress their own judgment to follow the crowd. And there is the "normality bias"—our tendency to believe that things will continue as they have been, even in the face of evidence to the contrary.

But perhaps most significant is what we might call the collective suspension of disbelief. Markets, after all, are not merely economic mechanisms; they are elaborate consensus realities. They function because we collectively agree they function. When that consensus begins to waver, it rarely announces itself with sirens and flashing lights. It manifests as a subtle shift in the atmosphere—a strange stillness in the air.

In late 1999, as the Dot-Com bubble approached its peak, Silicon Valley hummed with activity. Companies with no profits and questionable business models commanded billion-dollar valuations. Twenty-something entrepreneurs became paper millionaires overnight. The NASDAQ doubled in a single year.

Yet by December, something had changed. The language of infinite possibility had acquired a mechanical quality. The same phrases—"new paradigm," "network effects," "first-mover advantage"—repeated with religious fervor, as though repetition could make them more true. Venture capitalists still wrote checks, but with slightly more hesitation. IPO parties grew more lavish, as if to compensate for growing uncertainty.

The air had changed.

What makes these historical patterns relevant today is not that they predict specific outcomes, but that they illuminate the present. They remind us that economies are not abstract systems but human constructions, subject to human psychology. They show us that financial behavior follows emotional rhythms as much as rational calculations.

As we move through our current moment—with its AI enthusiasm, its cryptocurrency fluctuations, its post-pandemic recalibrations—we might ask ourselves: How does the air feel? What are we collectively choosing not to notice? What stories are we telling ourselves with increasing insistence?

This is not a call to panic or pessimism. Most shifts in economic weather bring rain to some and sunshine to others. The tulip bulb collapse created opportunities for Dutch merchants to redirect capital toward more productive trade. The dot-com crash cleared space for a more sustainable digital economy to emerge.

Rather, this is an invitation to awareness—to develop what our ancestors might have called weather-sense for economic conditions. To notice not just the data points and headlines, but the quality of the conversation, the emotional texture of financial decisions, the subtle signals that pass through crowds like a change in barometric pressure.

Because history rarely repeats itself exactly—but it often rhymes. And in those rhymes, in that poetry of human behavior across centuries, we can find not certainty, but perspective. Not predictions, but preparation.

Sometimes the most important economic indicator is simply this: a strange stillness in the air.

Chapter 2: When Optimism Feels Forced

There is a particular quality to the optimism that precedes economic collapse—a brittleness that reveals itself not in what is said, but in how it is said. The volume rises. The certainty hardens. The room for doubt narrows until it disappears entirely. What begins as genuine enthusiasm calcifies into something else: a performance of confidence that grows more strident as the foundations beneath it weaken.

In the spring of 1929, as stock prices climbed to unprecedented heights, the economist Irving Fisher famously declared that stocks had reached "a permanently high plateau." His words carried the weight of authority—Fisher was, after all, one of the most respected economists of his generation. What makes his declaration remarkable in retrospect is not merely that it was wrong, but that it came just months before the most devastating market crash in American history.

Fisher was not alone. Across the financial landscape that spring and summer, market commentators competed to outdo one another with bullish predictions. Newspaper headlines trumpeted new records. Investment newsletters dismissed concerns as the hand-wringing of pessimists who simply didn't understand the new economic order. The language of inevitability crept into financial discourse: this bull market wasn't just a temporary condition—it was the natural state of things.

When we look back at these pronouncements now, with the benefit of hindsight, what strikes us is their increasing desperation—as though each new declaration of confidence needed to be louder than the last to drown out the growing whispers of doubt.

This pattern repeats itself with remarkable consistency. In 1999, as the NASDAQ approached 5,000, technology analysts issued ever-higher price targets for companies that had never turned a profit. The rhetoric shifted from analysis to evangelism. Skeptics weren't just wrong—they were labeled as people who "didn't get it," who failed to understand the transformative nature of the internet. The language became quasi-religious: true believers versus heretics.

In 2007, as housing prices reached their apex, mortgage brokers, real estate agents, and financial commentators spoke with absolute certainty about the impossibility of a national housing downturn. "Real estate always goes up" became not just a slogan but an article of faith. Those who questioned this narrative were dismissed as lacking vision or, worse, trying to talk down a market that was delivering prosperity to millions.

What makes these periods of forced optimism so fascinating is how they reveal the social nature of economic confidence. Markets, after all, are not merely mechanisms for price discovery—they are complex human systems built on shared beliefs. When those beliefs begin to waver, the first response is rarely a reconsideration of assumptions. Instead, it's a doubling down, a collective insistence that everything remains fine.

This phenomenon has a name in psychology: preference falsification. Developed by the economist Timur Kuran, the concept describes situations where people publicly express views that differ from what they privately believe. In economic contexts, this often manifests as public expressions of confidence that mask private doubts.

Consider the investment banker who privately moves her personal portfolio to cash while publicly recommending aggressive stock purchases to clients. Or the real estate developer who begins quietly selling properties while telling reporters that the market has never been stronger. These contradictions between public statements and private actions often become visible only in retrospect, when journalists reconstruct the timeline of a collapse.

The forced quality of pre-crisis optimism also reveals itself in the treatment of dissenting voices. In healthy markets, skepticism is valued—it's part of the price discovery mechanism that makes markets efficient. But as bubbles inflate, skepticism becomes increasingly unwelcome. Dissenting analysts find themselves uninvited from conferences. Critical journalists struggle to get comments from industry leaders. Fund managers who express caution watch clients depart for more optimistic advisors.

This narrowing of acceptable opinion creates an information cascade. When people stop expressing doubts publicly, those doubts become invisible to others. The absence of visible concern is then interpreted as an absence of reasons for concern. The silence of skeptics becomes evidence for optimists that no legitimate skepticism exists.

We can see this dynamic clearly in the months before the 2008 financial crisis. Mortgage-backed securities received AAA ratings despite being built on increasingly questionable loans. Investment banks continued to market these instruments aggressively while simultaneously reducing their own exposure. Regulators, captured by the prevailing narrative of financial innovation, dismissed warnings about systemic risk.

The few voices that did express concern—economists like Nouriel Roubini and Robert Shiller, investors like Michael Burry—were labeled "Dr. Doom" or "permabears." Their warnings were acknowledged only to be immediately dismissed as implausible or exaggerated. The financial media, dependent on access to industry leaders and advertising dollars from financial institutions, largely amplified the optimistic consensus rather than investigating its foundations.

What makes forced optimism particularly dangerous is how it distorts our collective ability to process information. Evidence that supports the prevailing narrative gets amplified; evidence that contradicts it gets minimized or rationalized away. This selective attention creates a feedback loop where optimism becomes self-reinforcing, at least for a time.

Consider how rising prices themselves become evidence for further price increases. In the housing bubble, the fact that prices had been rising steadily for years was cited as proof that they would continue to rise. Historical patterns of reversion to the mean were dismissed with four dangerous words: "This time is different."

The quality of explanations changes during these periods as well. In the early stages of a bull market, optimism is usually grounded in concrete fundamentals: growing earnings, technological innovations, or policy changes. But as valuations stretch beyond what fundamentals can justify, explanations become more abstract, more theoretical, more detached from measurable reality.

In the dot-com boom, this manifested as metrics like "eyeballs" and "mindshare" replacing traditional measures such as revenue and profit. In the housing bubble, it appeared as increasingly exotic financial instruments that few understood but many trusted. In cryptocurrency markets, it emerged as appeals to concepts like "digital scarcity" and "decentralization" to justify astronomical valuations for tokens with no clear utility.

This shift from concrete to abstract reasoning isn't merely an intellectual curiosity—it's a warning sign. When the justification for an investment becomes primarily theoretical rather than practical, when the timeframe for realizing returns stretches from the immediate to the indefinite future, when success depends on everyone agreeing to believe the same story—these are the conditions under which forced optimism flourishes.

Yet even as public discourse becomes increasingly detached from reality, individuals begin to sense the disconnect. This creates a curious phenomenon where people simultaneously participate in the collective narrative while harboring private doubts. The investment manager who tells clients to stay fully invested while increasing her personal cash position. The homebuyer who stretches to purchase a house while worrying it might be the peak of the market. The tech worker who accepts stock options while quietly diversifying his portfolio.

This tension between public expression and private doubt creates the particular atmosphere that precedes economic crisis—a social environment where optimism is both ubiquitous and fragile, where confidence is loudly proclaimed but quietly questioned. It produces what we might call the "emperor's new clothes effect," where many people suspect the prevailing narrative is false but hesitate to be the first to say so.

The most telling sign of forced optimism may be the emotional response to questioning. In healthy markets, skeptical questions are met with thoughtful answers. In bubble markets, they're met with indignation, dismissal, or accusations of disloyalty. When "Are you with us or against us?" becomes the response to legitimate concerns, when optimism becomes not just an outlook but an identity, when questioning the narrative feels like a social transgression—these are the moments when we should listen most carefully to our doubts.

For it is precisely when optimism cannot tolerate questioning that it has transformed from genuine confidence into something more brittle and dangerous: a collective performance that continues only because no one wants to be the first to stop applauding.

Chapter 3: The Stories We Tell Ourselves

There is perhaps no force more powerful in markets—or in human society—than a well-crafted narrative. When we examine the quiet periods before economic storms, we find not just numbers shifting on balance sheets, but stories taking hold in the collective imagination.

These are not mere tales. They are the frameworks through which we understand our place in the economic universe. They tell us what to value, what to fear, what to desire, and most importantly, what to believe is possible.

Consider how we speak of markets: they "recover," they "struggle," they "rally," they show "strength" or "weakness." We have anthropomorphized a vast system of human exchange into a character with moods and intentions. This is not a linguistic accident. It reflects our deep need to create order from complexity, to find agency where there may be only emergence.

In the calm before economic storms, certain stories gain particular power. Let me share three that appear with remarkable consistency throughout history.

—-

The first is what we might call the "New Era" narrative. It appears in virtually every bubble, though its particulars change. In 1720, it was the story that the South Sea Company would generate unimaginable wealth from South American trade. In 1929, it was that a modern industrial economy had permanently conquered the business cycle. In 1999, it was that the internet would render traditional business metrics obsolete.

The New Era story always contains the same essential claim: "This time is different." The old rules no longer apply. The constraints that limited past generations have been transcended. The future will not resemble the past.

What makes these narratives so seductive is that they contain elements of truth. The railroad did transform commerce. The internet did revolutionize information flow. Artificial intelligence is changing how we work. But the story becomes dangerous when it suggests that fundamental principles of economics, human psychology, or risk have somehow been suspended.

Irving Fisher, perhaps America's most respected economist, declared in October 1929 that stock prices had reached "what looks like a permanently high plateau." Nine days later, the market began its catastrophic collapse. Fisher was not a fool—he was a brilliant man caught in a compelling narrative.

—-

The second recurring story is what we might call the "Virtuous Expert" narrative. This is the belief that somewhere, people with superior knowledge and authority are ensuring our collective safety.

In the mid-2000s, this manifested as faith in the Federal Reserve's ability to manage any economic disruption. Alan Greenspan was nicknamed "The Maestro," as though the economy were an orchestra that could be conducted with precision. When questioned about the housing market's sustainability in 2005, he acknowledged "froth" but denied any national bubble could exist.

The Virtuous Expert story provides profound psychological comfort. It allows us to participate in increasingly risky behavior while believing that someone wiser is watching over the system. It transforms uncertainty into delegated responsibility. We need not understand the complexities ourselves; others have it under control.

This narrative persists despite repeated historical evidence that experts, however well-intentioned and credentialed, suffer from the same cognitive biases as everyone else. They too can be captured by prevailing stories. They too can mistake the map for the territory.

—-

The third story, perhaps most powerful of all, is what we might call the "Inevitable Prosperity" narrative. This is the belief that despite short-term fluctuations, the arc of markets bends toward growth and abundance.

This story draws strength from genuine historical patterns. Indeed, over long time horizons, economies have grown, technologies have advanced, and living standards have improved. But the narrative becomes dangerous when it suggests this trajectory is smooth or guaranteed, particularly in the short term.

During the housing boom of the early 2000s, the Inevitable Prosperity narrative appeared in the common wisdom that "real estate always goes up." This wasn't just an investment thesis—it became an article of faith, a story about how the world fundamentally works.

What makes this narrative particularly powerful is that it aligns with our deepest hopes. We want to believe in progress. We want to believe that our investments will grow, that our children will prosper, that the future will be better than the past. And in the longest view, these hopes have often been realized. But the path has never been straight, and the timeline never certain.

—-

These stories gain strength from their social nature. They are not merely ideas we consider in isolation—they are frameworks we share, discuss, and reinforce through conversation. When your neighbor, your financial advisor, and the financial media all reference the same narrative, it creates a powerful consensus reality that becomes increasingly difficult to question.

As the writer Upton Sinclair observed: "It is difficult to get a man to understand something when his salary depends upon his not understanding it." We might add that it is equally difficult to get someone to question a story when their sense of security, identity, and future depends upon believing it.

The most dangerous moment comes when these narratives harden from hypotheses into dogma. Questions become heresies. Skepticism becomes disloyalty. The story no longer describes reality—it replaces it.

And here we find the central paradox of the calm before the storm: the stronger the narrative becomes, the more it diverges from underlying realities, the more energy builds in the system. Like a fault line where pressure accumulates before an earthquake, the tension between story and reality grows until something must give.

—-

This is not to suggest that all economic narratives are false or dangerous. Stories are essential tools for making sense of complex systems. We cannot navigate markets—or life—without them. The question is not whether we use narratives, but whether our narratives remain flexible, open to revision, and grounded in observable reality.

In the quiet times before market disruptions, pay attention not just to what stories are being told, but how they are being told. Watch for narratives that brook no disagreement, that dismiss contradictory evidence, that explain away warning signs with increasingly elaborate justifications.

Listen for the moment when "this investment has potential" transforms into "only a fool would miss this opportunity." Notice when "the data suggests" becomes "everyone knows." These subtle shifts in language reflect deeper shifts in collective thinking, the hardening of fluid possibility into brittle certainty.

The most resilient investors and institutions maintain what the psychologist Philip Tetlock calls "active open-mindedness"—the willingness to consider alternative perspectives, to update beliefs based on new information, to hold multiple possible futures in mind simultaneously. They use stories as tools rather than truths.

For it is in the space between absolute certainty and complete doubt that wisdom resides—a space that narrows dramatically in the deceptive calm before economic storms.

Chapter 4: The Seduction of Stability

There is something hypnotic about calm waters. Stand at the edge of a still lake at dawn, and you'll find your breathing slowing to match its glassy surface. The human mind craves this kind of stability—this reassurance that the world around us is predictable, manageable, and known.

Financial markets offer their own version of this seduction. After periods of sustained growth, a peculiar psychological state emerges among investors, economists, and ordinary citizens alike. It's not merely optimism, but something deeper: a collective belief in the permanence of stability itself. We begin to mistake the absence of volatility for the absence of risk.

Consider the five-year period before the 2008 financial crisis. Economists spoke of "The Great Moderation"—a term coined to describe an era when economic fluctuations had supposedly been tamed through sophisticated monetary policy and financial innovation. Volatility in markets had declined to historically low levels. Housing prices followed a steady upward trajectory that seemed as reliable as sunrise. The Federal Reserve, under Alan Greenspan and then Ben Bernanke, projected an aura of mastery over economic forces.

This perceived stability wasn't imaginary. By many conventional measures, the economy was indeed functioning smoothly. Inflation remained low. Unemployment seemed manageable. The yield curve—that mysterious oracle of bond markets—signaled no immediate dangers. The system appeared to have achieved a kind of equilibrium.

But stability, when it persists too long, creates its own vulnerabilities.

—

In ecology, scientists have observed a phenomenon called the "stability-complexity spiral." As an ecosystem becomes more stable, its inhabitants gradually lose their adaptability. Species that evolved during periods of fluctuation and stress begin to specialize, optimizing for the current conditions rather than maintaining resilience against change. The forest that has gone too long without a cleansing fire becomes dangerously overgrown. The river that hasn't flooded in decades sees development creep into its natural floodplain.

Financial systems follow a similar pattern. During periods of stability, financial institutions gradually increase their leverage. Risk management models, calibrated on recent data, begin to underestimate the probability of extreme events. Correlations that held true during normal times are assumed to be universal laws. The system becomes simultaneously more complex and more brittle.

As Hyman Minsky observed in his Financial Instability Hypothesis, stability itself breeds instability. The longer a period of calm persists, the more market participants take on speculative positions that depend on that calm continuing indefinitely.

"The success of a capitalist economy," Minsky wrote, "depends upon the ability of financial institutions to innovate and adapt as the economy evolves." But innovation without occasional correction leads to excess. Safety gives birth to recklessness.

—

The human dimension of this pattern is equally important. Extended periods of stability create a form of collective amnesia. The institutional memory of previous crises fades. The cautious old guard retires, replaced by a new generation that has known only success. Risk managers who raise concerns are marginalized as unnecessarily conservative, failing to understand the "new paradigm."

During the housing boom of the early 2000s, mortgage brokers who had never seen a nationwide housing decline confidently asserted that "real estate always goes up." Their belief wasn't entirely irrational—they were working from the data available to them, from their lived experience. The last nationwide housing decline had occurred before many of them were born.

This amnesia extends beyond professional circles. Ordinary citizens, too, begin to take stability for granted. Retirement plans assume historical returns will continue uninterrupted. Household savings rates decline as prosperity seems assured. The psychological buffer against hard times—both financial and emotional—gradually erodes.

We see this pattern repeatedly throughout history. In the 1920s, the phrase "permanent plateau of prosperity" captured the zeitgeist just before the crash. In the late 1990s, the "new economy" would supposedly render business cycles obsolete. In 2006, the sophisticated risk management of modern banking was thought to have distributed risk so efficiently that systemic collapse was virtually impossible.

—-

The seduction of stability operates on multiple levels simultaneously. At the individual level, it manifests as complacency—a relaxation of vigilance. At the institutional level, it appears as increased leverage and reduced safety margins. At the regulatory level, it emerges as a willingness to deregulate, to remove the guardrails established during previous crises.

Perhaps most insidiously, stability changes our relationship with time itself. The recent past becomes our reference point for normalcy. We begin to see the stable period not as one phase in an ongoing cycle, but as the natural state of affairs—the way things are supposed to be.

This temporal distortion affects our ability to properly assess risk. A financial innovation that has performed well for five years is deemed "proven." A trading strategy that has generated consistent returns is considered "reliable." The absence of problems becomes evidence that problems cannot occur, rather than a warning that problems have been deferred.

In his book "Fooled by Randomness," Nassim Taleb illustrates this concept with a simple thought experiment. Imagine a game where you have a 99% chance of making a small profit and a 1% chance of a catastrophic loss. If you play this game daily, you might experience years of steady gains before encountering the ruinous outcome. During those years, it would be easy to convince yourself that your strategy is sound, that you possess special skill or insight. The stability of your returns would seem to confirm your approach.

But that stability would be an illusion—a statistical artifact that masks the true nature of the risk you're taking.

—-

The most dangerous aspect of stability's seduction is how it undermines our ability to imagine alternatives. As the memory of previous crises fades, our capacity for envisioning potential future crises atrophies as well. The range of outcomes we consider plausible narrows. Extreme scenarios are dismissed as alarmist fantasy rather than treated as remote but real possibilities.

This narrowing of imagination affects even sophisticated risk managers. Financial models built during stable periods typically underestimate the probability of extreme events and the correlation between different assets during times of stress. The mathematical term for this is "fat tails"—the tendency of real-world financial data to produce extreme outcomes more frequently than normal distributions would predict.

But the problem isn't merely technical. It's deeply human. We struggle to maintain emotional preparedness for events we haven't personally experienced. We dismiss warnings about unfamiliar threats. We convince ourselves that the stability we currently enjoy is deserved, earned, and therefore permanent.

And so the quiet before the storm becomes quieter still. Warnings are dismissed. Precautions are deemed excessive. The few voices expressing concern are drowned out by the comfortable consensus. The water remains glassy and still, reflecting a perfect blue sky—even as barometric pressure drops and distant clouds gather on the horizon.

This is the paradox at the heart of economic cycles: the very success of the system in creating stability undermines the conditions that made that stability possible. Like the forest that grows too thick without occasional fire, the financial system becomes increasingly vulnerable precisely when it appears most robust.

The seduction of stability isn't a failure of intelligence. It's a feature of human psychology—our tendency to normalize our current circumstances, to find patterns even in randomness, to prefer comfortable illusions over uncomfortable uncertainties. It affects the brilliant and the ordinary alike. It operates in boardrooms and living rooms, in regulatory agencies and trading floors.

And it ensures that when the storm finally breaks, it will always come as a surprise.

Chapter 5: Why Warnings Are Ignored

There is a peculiar quality to human attention in the years before economic collapse. It resembles the selective hearing that parents develop—able to sleep through traffic noise but instantly alert to a child's faintest cry. In financial markets, this selective attention works in reverse: we become hypersensitive to confirming evidence while developing an impressive capacity to sleep through alarms.

In the autumn of 2006, economist Nouriel Roubini stood before an audience at the International Monetary Fund and predicted that the American housing market would soon collapse, triggering a severe recession. His colleagues nicknamed him "Dr. Doom." The financial press treated his warnings as the eccentric views of a perpetual pessimist. Eighteen months later, as his predictions materialized with devastating precision, the same publications would describe him as "prophetic."

This pattern—the dismissal of accurate warnings followed by their posthumous celebration—appears with such consistency throughout financial history that we must ask: Why do we ignore the voices that, in retrospect, spoke the truth?

The answer lies not in a failure of information but in the architecture of collective belief.

—-

Consider the fate of warnings before the 1929 crash. In early 1928, Paul M. Warburg, a respected banker who helped create the Federal Reserve System, publicly cautioned that unchecked speculation would lead to "a general depression involving the entire country." The market's response was swift—not in corrective action, but in attacking Warburg himself. The *Commercial & Financial Chronicle* dismissed his concerns as "antiquated" thinking that failed to appreciate the modern economy's resilience.

When Roger Babson predicted the crash in September 1929, stating that "factories will shut down... men will be thrown out of work," the *Wall Street Journal* responded with an editorial titled "A Babson Break," mocking his "habitual pessimism." The market rose further, seemingly invalidating his warning, before collapsing just weeks later.

What makes these warnings so easy to dismiss?

—-

First, warnings violate what psychologists call the "affect heuristic"—our tendency to judge risk through our emotional state. During periods of rising markets, collective emotion turns increasingly positive. Warnings create cognitive dissonance, an uncomfortable clash between the pleasant feeling of prosperity and the anxiety of potential loss. The easiest resolution to this dissonance is not to adjust our beliefs, but to discredit the source of discomfort.

Second, warnings are rarely delivered with precision timing. They typically arrive too early—sometimes years before the actual crisis. The longer a warning goes unfulfilled, the easier it becomes to dismiss. Paul Warburg's 1928 cautions appeared premature for over a year before vindication. By then, his credibility had already suffered significant damage.

Third, and perhaps most importantly, warnings threaten what sociologist Pierre Bourdieu called "social capital"—the relationships, status, and belonging that form our place in community. During market euphoria, expressing doubt becomes a social transgression. The warning-giver is not merely predicting economic events but violating the unspoken rules of collective optimism.

—-

In January 2007, economist Robert Shiller—who had accurately warned of both the dot-com bubble and the housing bubble—appeared on CNBC. The host introduced him as "the fellow who keeps warning about a housing bubble," with a tone suggesting both amusement and dismissal. When Shiller explained his concerns about housing prices, another guest interrupted: "You've been saying this for years, and yet prices keep going up."

The exchange perfectly captured the social mechanism of warning dismissal. The warning-giver becomes defined not by the content of their warning but by their violation of optimistic consensus. They are cast not as analysts but as characters—the perpetual bear, the broken clock, the attention-seeker.

This characterization serves a protective function. If warnings come from people who can be dismissed as constitutionally pessimistic, then the warnings themselves need not be evaluated on merit.

—

The most effective dismissal of warnings, however, comes not through direct confrontation but through subtle marginalization. Before the 2008 crisis, many economists expressed concerns about housing prices and household debt levels in academic papers and specialized publications. These warnings weren't actively refuted; they were simply never amplified. They remained confined to footnotes and specialist discussions, never reaching the threshold of general attention.

This process of marginalization follows predictable patterns. Warnings that come from outside established institutions are dismissed as uninformed. Warnings from insiders are attributed to personal or political motives. Technical warnings are deemed too complex for practical relevance. Simple warnings are characterized as oversimplified.

The financial system thus creates what sociologists call a "structural silence"—not an active conspiracy of suppression, but a distributed system where incentives at every level favor the quiet burial of uncomfortable insights.

—-

The most tragic aspect of warning dismissal is that it often happens within the mind of the warning-giver themselves. Internal risk managers at financial institutions before 2008 frequently identified excessive leverage and questionable mortgage practices. Many chose to modulate their concerns or keep them private, understanding the professional consequences of persistent alarm-raising.

As one former risk officer at a major investment bank later testified: "I began to feel like the boy who cried wolf. After the third or fourth time your concerns are dismissed, you begin to doubt yourself. You wonder if you're missing something that everyone else sees."

This self-censorship completes the cycle of warning dismissal. External critics are marginalized while internal doubts are suppressed, creating the illusion of consensus where none truly exists.

—-

There is a deeper psychological dynamic at work in our dismissal of warnings—one that connects to our relationship with uncertainty itself. Warnings force us to hold two contradictory possibilities in mind simultaneously: the comfortable present and a threatening future. This cognitive state, which psychologists call "ambiguity," creates profound discomfort.

Studies show that most people will choose a certain negative outcome over an ambiguous situation with both better and worse possible outcomes. We prefer the devil we know. Financial warnings create precisely this uncomfortable ambiguity—the possibility that our prosperity might be illusory, that the future might not resemble the present.

In dismissing warnings, we are not merely protecting our financial positions or social standing. We are protecting our sense of a knowable, predictable world.

—

The dismissal of warnings creates a dangerous feedback loop. As accurate warnings go unheeded, those who issued them either fall silent or escalate their rhetoric to break through the indifference. This escalation makes their warnings sound increasingly extreme, which further marginalizes them. Meanwhile, those who dismissed previous warnings feel validated by their continued prosperity, becoming even more resistant to future cautions.

This dynamic explains why warnings often seem to come only from the margins—from eccentric personalities, retired officials no longer concerned with institutional standing, or those with little to lose. The center grows increasingly quiet as the periphery grows increasingly strident.

By the time a bubble reaches its final stages, warning and dismissal no longer engage in genuine dialogue. They speak past each other in entirely different languages.

—

What might we learn from this pattern? Not that we should heed every warning—false alarms are plentiful in financial markets. Rather, we might develop a more nuanced relationship with warning itself.

The most valuable approach treats warnings neither as prophecies to be believed nor annoyances to be dismissed, but as alternative scenarios to be seriously considered. This requires what psychologist Philip Tetlock calls "active open-mindedness"—the willingness to detach our identity from our predictions, to hold contradictory possibilities in mind simultaneously.

The Japanese concept of *nemawashi*—the practice of speaking with all stakeholders before making decisions—offers a model. In traditional Japanese organizations, concerns are actively solicited rather than reluctantly tolerated. The person who identifies potential problems is not a troublemaker but a contributor to collective wisdom.

—

Perhaps the most important insight about warnings comes from understanding their emotional nature. Warnings are not merely intellectual propositions; they are invitations to anxiety. Our dismissal of them is not merely cognitive error but emotional self-protection.

This suggests that creating more resilient financial systems requires not just better information but better emotional capacity—the ability to face anxiety without immediately suppressing it. The organizations and societies that best navigate uncertainty are not those that generate the most optimistic predictions, but those that can hold the tension of conflicting possibilities without premature resolution.

In the quiet that precedes financial storms, warnings whisper all around us. They speak not just in dramatic pronouncements from notable economists, but in subtle contradictions, in small facts that don't align with the dominant narrative, in questions that receive no satisfactory answers.

The challenge is not merely to hear these warnings, but to create cultures where they can be spoken and received without the speaker being cast out and without the listener being overwhelmed—where the discomfort they bring is recognized not as a threat to our well-being, but as essential to preserving it.

Chapter 6: Tulip Mania: Beauty at Any Price

In the winter of 1636, in the prosperous Dutch Republic, a single tulip bulb—specifically, a rare variety called Semper Augustus with its distinctive flame-like red streaks on white petals—changed hands for a price that could have purchased one of Amsterdam's grandest canal houses. This was not an isolated transaction between eccentric collectors. It represented the pinnacle of what we now call Tulip Mania, the first documented financial bubble in modern history.

What makes this episode so enduring in our collective memory is not merely its absurdity—though there is certainly absurdity in the notion of trading a flower bulb for the equivalent of a mansion. Rather, it is because tulip mania offers us a pristine example of how human psychology transforms objects from things of beauty into vessels of speculative desire.

The tulip arrived in Western Europe from the Ottoman Empire in the mid-16th century. For the Dutch, these flowers represented more than exotic beauty. They arrived at a pivotal moment when the young republic was establishing itself as a global trading power. The Netherlands had recently won independence from Spain and was experiencing unprecedented prosperity. The merchant class was expanding, and with new wealth came new forms of status display.

What began as genuine appreciation for the tulip's aesthetic qualities gradually shifted into something else entirely. The rarest varieties—those with vivid "broken" patterns caused, ironically, by a mosaic virus that weakened the plant—commanded the highest prices. The Semper Augustus, the Admirael van Enkhuizen, the Viceroy—these names became as familiar to Dutch traders as blue-chip stocks are to today's investors.

By 1636, tulips were no longer being purchased primarily to be planted and admired. Instead, they became abstract financial instruments. Most bulbs traded during the height of the mania never left the ground. They existed as notations in contracts, changing ownership multiple times during their dormant winter season before they could even be dug up.

The market developed its own infrastructure with surprising speed. Taverns became informal exchanges where tulip traders gathered. Contracts were standardized. Credit was extended. Options trading emerged, allowing speculators to purchase the right to buy bulbs at a future date without putting up the full price. These financial innovations—remarkably sophisticated for their time—accelerated the bubble's inflation.

What makes this period so instructive is how it reveals the social dimensions of market psychology. The mania spread through networks of family and friends. It crossed class boundaries, drawing in not just wealthy merchants but also shopkeepers, craftsmen, farmers, and sailors. Contemporary accounts describe maids investing their savings and farmers neglecting their fields to speculate in tulips. When enough people believe in rising prices, belief itself becomes temporarily self-fulfilling.

Yet throughout this frenzy, there were quiet voices of concern. Some Dutch citizens wrote pamphlets warning of the unsustainability of tulip prices. Religious leaders preached against the moral hazards of speculation. These warnings were largely ignored or ridiculed—a pattern we will see repeated in every subsequent bubble.

By February 1637, the market collapsed virtually overnight. Buyers simply stopped appearing at the auctions in Haarlem, Amsterdam, and other trading centers. The precise trigger remains unclear—perhaps nothing more than a critical mass of doubt. What is clear is the aftermath: contracts went unfulfilled, debts unpaid, and many speculators were financially ruined. The Dutch government eventually intervened, allowing contracts to be voided upon payment of a small percentage of their face value.

The psychological whiplash was severe. What had been viewed as a legitimate investment opportunity was suddenly seen as foolish gambling. Those who had boasted of their tulip profits now denied ever participating. The very word "tulip" became synonymous with foolishness and delusion.

Yet it would be a mistake to view the participants simply as irrational. From within the bubble, their behavior made a kind of sense. When everyone around you confirms that tulip bulbs are valuable investments, when you witness others making fortunes, when respected members of society participate openly, the truly irrational choice seems to be staying out of the market.

This is the subtle power of market psychology—it transforms the absurd into the reasonable through social consensus. The tulip was never just a flower; it became a vessel for Dutch aspirations, a symbol of prosperity, a ticket to social mobility. Its price reflected not its intrinsic value as a plant but its value as a social and financial signifier.

The calm that preceded the tulip market's collapse had its own distinctive quality. Contemporary accounts describe a strange confidence in late 1636, even as prices reached levels that, in retrospect, were obviously unsustainable. There was a collective holding of breath, a sense that while everyone understood the situation couldn't continue forever, no one wanted to be the first to acknowledge it.

What makes Tulip Mania so valuable as a historical case study is its clarity. Unlike modern financial instruments with their layers of complexity, the tulip bulb is refreshingly straightforward. Either its price reflects its value as a flower, or it doesn't. When a Semper Augustus bulb costs as much as a house, the disconnection between price and intrinsic value becomes impossible to rationalize—at least in retrospect.

Yet this same pattern—the transformation of an object from a thing valued for its inherent qualities into a pure speculative vehicle—repeats throughout history. The tulip teaches us that humans don't just value things for what they are, but for what we collectively agree they represent. And when that collective agreement shifts, as it inevitably must when disconnected from fundamental reality, the result is not a gentle correction but a sudden collapse.

The tulip fields of Holland still bloom each spring, drawing tourists from around the world. They serve as living reminders that beauty has its own authentic value—one that persists long after the speculative fever breaks, after the last contract is settled, after the last debt is paid or forgiven. The tulip survived its mania. The question that echoes through financial history is whether we, as market participants, ever truly learn from such episodes, or whether we are destined to rediscover these lessons with each new generation, with each new object of desire.

Chapter 7: The South Sea Bubble: Promises Made of Air

In the spring of 1720, London hummed with a peculiar energy. Carriages crowded the narrow streets of Exchange Alley, depositing nobles alongside shopkeepers. Ladies in fine silk dresses stood shoulder to shoulder with laborers in rough cotton. They gathered not for a royal procession or public execution, but for something far more intoxicating: the opportunity to purchase shares in the South Sea Company.

Inside coffee houses that doubled as informal trading floors, the air hung thick with tobacco smoke and whispered fortunes. Transactions were recorded on scraps of paper, handshakes sealed deals worth thousands of pounds, and rumors traveled faster than truth. This was not merely a financial event—it was theater, romance, and religion combined.

"The entire nation has become a corporation of traders," wrote one contemporary observer. "From the apprentice to the aristocrat, all thoughts are directed to the rising of stocks."

The South Sea Bubble represents a crucial evolutionary step in our understanding of financial manias. While the Tulipmania centered on physical objects—however impractical—the South Sea Company traded almost purely in narratives, expectations, and dreams. It was capitalism's first great experiment with selling the future.

—-

The South Sea Company was established in 1711, during a period when Britain was financially exhausted from the War of Spanish Succession. The company's founding purpose seemed legitimate enough: it received monopoly rights to trade with Spanish colonies in South America in exchange for assuming a portion of Britain's war debt. The arrangement appealed to the government, which could convert its unwieldy debt into company stock, and to investors, who saw potential in new markets.

There was, however, a fundamental problem that few acknowledged: Spain severely restricted foreign trade with its colonies, rendering the company's supposed commercial advantage largely theoretical. The South Sea Company conducted only one trading voyage in its first seven years.

But this practical limitation hardly mattered. The company's true product was not goods from the New World, but financial engineering—a concept so new that few could properly evaluate it. In 1719, the company proposed an audacious scheme: it would take over the entire British national debt, converting government annuities into company shares. Parliament approved the plan in 1720, setting the stage for what would follow.

John Blunt, the company's director, understood something profound about human psychology: when a financial proposition is complex enough, people evaluate it not on its details but on the confidence with which it is presented. The South Sea directors projected unwavering assurance. They spoke of the "inexhaustible wealth" of South American trade while deliberately keeping operational details vague.

"There was genius in this vagueness," wrote economic historian Charles Mackay decades later. "It allowed each investor to project their own fantasies onto the enterprise."

—-

The initial stock offering in April 1720 was priced at £300 per share. By June, the price had reached £700. By August, it approached £1,000—a more than tripling in four months. What fueled this extraordinary rise? Not profits or dividends, which remained negligible, but a carefully orchestrated campaign of hype and manipulation.

The company lent money to investors to buy shares, accepting those same shares as collateral—creating a circular system where rising prices generated more buying power. Directors spread rumors of imminent trade concessions from Spain that never materialized. Politicians who received preferential share allocations became enthusiastic public advocates. The company even paid people to be visibly excited about their investments in public spaces.

"There grew a strange new profession in London," noted one diarist. "Men who would position themselves in coffee houses and speak loudly of their South Sea profits, only to vanish when questioned about specifics."

As share prices rose, the phenomenon became self-reinforcing. People who had initially scoffed at the company watched their more adventurous friends and neighbors grow paper-rich. The fear of missing out—that most reliable of human anxieties—drove even skeptics into the market. When Sir Isaac Newton, perhaps the greatest scientific mind of the era, was asked about the sustainability of South Sea shares, he reportedly said, "I can calculate the motion of heavenly bodies, but not the madness of people."

Yet even Newton eventually succumbed, investing a substantial sum and ultimately losing £20,000—equivalent to millions in today's currency.

—-

The South Sea mania inspired dozens of imitators. In a phenomenon that would be familiar to observers of the 1990s dot-com boom or the 2017 cryptocurrency surge, new companies formed overnight, each promising revolutionary business models with minimal detail. These became known as "bubble companies."

One proposed to import walnut trees from Virginia. Another claimed it would manufacture a perpetual motion machine. Most infamous was "a company for carrying on an undertaking of great advantage, but nobody to know what it is." Its founder collected £2,000 in subscription fees in a single morning before disappearing forever.

Parliament, belatedly recognizing the danger, passed the "Bubble Act" in June 1720, requiring all joint-stock companies to have royal charters. Ironically, this legislation, intended to curb speculation, was actually promoted by South Sea directors to eliminate competition for investment capital.

The bubble reached its zenith in August 1720. The precise trigger for its collapse remains debated, but like all financial manias, it ultimately faced the constraint that indefinite exponential growth is impossible. The company had promised dividends it could not possibly deliver. The gap between narrative and reality had stretched beyond breaking point.

When selling began, it accelerated with the same psychological momentum that had driven prices upward. By December, South Sea shares had returned to their starting price. By the following year, they were nearly worthless.

—

The aftermath revealed extensive corruption. Government officials had accepted bribes. Company books had been falsified. Insiders had sold their shares near the peak while encouraging public buying. The scandal reached into Parliament and even touched the king's circle. The Chancellor of the Exchequer was imprisoned in the Tower of London. Several company directors had their estates confiscated.

For ordinary investors, there was little recourse. Many families of moderate means who had converted their life savings into South Sea shares found themselves destitute. The national mood turned from euphoria to bitter anger. Pamphlets and broadsides depicted the company directors as devils leading the innocent to slaughter.

"The South Sea Bubble demonstrated something profound about financial markets," wrote Adam Smith fifty years later. "That the collective imagination, when properly stimulated, can create value from nothing—and then return it to nothing just as quickly."

—-

What makes the South Sea Bubble particularly instructive is how it established patterns that would repeat throughout financial history. It revealed the dangerous alchemy that occurs when financial innovation outpaces regulatory understanding. It demonstrated how political connections can be monetized through preferential access to investments. Most importantly, it showed how a compelling narrative can temporarily suspend normal critical judgment.

The South Sea Company never delivered on its promises of South American trade. It never generated significant commercial profits. What it sold, essentially, was a story—a story about future wealth, about Britain's expanding global influence, about the transformative power of financial innovation.

For a brief moment, that story seemed more valuable than the solid realities of land, labor, and physical goods. When confidence in the story faltered, the elaborate structure collapsed.

Three hundred years later, we still struggle with the lessons of the South Sea Bubble. We have built more sophisticated markets, more complex regulations, more nuanced understanding of financial psychology. Yet time and again, we find ourselves captivated by promises made of air—whether internet companies without profits, cryptocurrencies without use cases, or AI ventures without proven business models.

The quiet that precedes these storms always feels different from previous episodes. There are always reasonable-sounding arguments for why "this time is different." But beneath the specifics, the human psychology remains remarkably constant: our desire to believe in financial alchemy, our susceptibility to confident narratives, and our eternal hope that wealth can be created through consensus rather than through the slower, harder work of creating actual value.

As we move from the South Sea Bubble to the Roaring Twenties in our next chapter, we will see how these same psychological patterns manifested in a more modern context, with different technologies but familiar human emotions driving the cycle of euphoria and collapse.

Chapter 8: The Roaring Twenties: Champagne Before Collapse

There is a particular quality to the air just before a thunderstorm—a stillness, a heaviness, an electric charge that makes the hairs on your arms stand up. Animals grow quiet. The wind pauses. And in that suspended moment, everything feels both intensely present and somehow unreal.

The 1920s in America carried that same atmospheric quality. The decade glittered with an almost supernatural brightness, a champagne bubble of prosperity that seemed as if it would never pop. It was a period so defined by its exuberance that we still call it "Roaring"—a word that suggests not just noise but a kind of triumphant, leonine confidence.

"We in America today are nearer to the final triumph over poverty than ever before in the history of any land," declared Herbert Hoover in August 1928, not long before accepting the Republican nomination for president. "The poorhouse is vanishing from among us."

Such was the spirit of the age—a conviction that America had entered a new era where economic hardship would become a relic, like the horse and buggy or gas-lit streets. But like all moments of supreme confidence, the Roaring Twenties contained within them the seeds of their own undoing. The champagne was flowing, but few noticed the hairline cracks forming in the crystal glasses that held it.

—-

The story of the 1920s begins, as many American stories do, with technology. The mass production of automobiles, telephones, radios, and household appliances transformed daily life and created new industries seemingly overnight. In 1919, there were 6.7 million cars on American roads. By 1929, there were 23 million—nearly one for every household in America. Radio ownership exploded from almost nothing to 10 million sets by the decade's end. Electricity reached into homes that had known only kerosene and candles.

This technological revolution drove an economic boom unlike anything the nation had experienced. Between 1922 and 1929, the Dow Jones Industrial Average rose 497 percent. Manufacturing output increased by 64 percent. For the first time in American history, a substantial middle class emerged with disposable income and access to consumer credit.

"Buy now, pay later" became the mantra of the age. Installment plans allowed ordinary Americans to purchase cars, refrigerators, and radios they couldn't afford outright. By 1929, 60 percent of cars and 80 percent of radios were bought on credit. Consumer debt nearly doubled during the decade.

Meanwhile, a new financial culture was taking hold. Before the 1920s, the stock market had been largely the province of professional investors and the wealthy. But as prosperity spread, so did stock ownership. The number of shareholders grew from fewer than 2 million in 1920 to over 10 million by 1929. Newspapers published stock tables; barbers and taxi drivers traded tips on hot stocks; investment trusts (the mutual funds of their day) proliferated.

"Everyone ought to be rich," proclaimed John J. Raskob, a General Motors executive, in a 1929 Ladies Home Journal article. He outlined how anyone could become wealthy by investing just $15 a month in common stocks. The article appeared in August 1929, two months before the crash.

—

But beneath the champagne surface, the economic foundation was developing structural weaknesses. The prosperity of the 1920s was remarkably uneven. While the top 1 percent saw their incomes rise by 75 percent during the decade, the bottom 93 percent experienced much more modest gains. By 1929, the richest 24,000 families in America had an income equal to that of the 11.5 million poorest families.

Agriculture, which still employed a quarter of American workers, languished in a depression throughout the decade. Farmers who had expanded production during World War I faced collapsing prices afterward. Farm foreclosures became common; rural banks failed at alarming rates. Coal mining, textiles, and other traditional industries similarly struggled while new consumer industries boomed.

This imbalance created a fundamental problem: production capacity was outstripping consumers' ability to purchase goods. As economist Waddill Catchings warned in 1927, "We can produce more than we can consume... There is almost no limit to our capacity to produce goods, but there is a very definite limit to our capacity to consume them."

The solution, temporarily, was credit—the "buy now, pay later" approach that kept the economic engine running. But debt can only stretch so far before it must be repaid or defaulted upon.

Meanwhile, the Federal Reserve, still a relatively new institution, made a critical error. Concerned about speculation in the stock market, the Fed raised interest rates in 1928 and 1929, hoping to cool what its members saw as an overheated market. Instead, the higher rates attracted more foreign money into American stocks while simultaneously putting pressure on the real economy.

—-

The market's rise seemed to defy gravity—and the warnings of skeptics. In March 1929, Paul Warburg, a respected banker who had helped design the Federal Reserve System, cautioned that unchecked speculation would lead to "a general depression involving the entire country." The commercial and financial chronicle dismissed him as "a Cassandra in Wall Street."

Roger Babson, an eccentric but respected statistician, had been predicting a crash since 1926. "Sooner or later a crash is coming, and it may be terrific," he warned again in September 1929. The next day, the New York Times reported that his comments had caused a temporary dip in stocks—what became known as the "Babson Break"—but the market quickly recovered. Wall Street's leading economists rushed to reassure investors.

"Stock prices have reached what looks like a permanently high plateau," declared Yale economist Irving Fisher on October 17, 1929, in perhaps the most infamous economic prediction in American history.

Fisher was not alone. The Harvard Economic Society assured investors that "a severe depression like that of 1920-21 is outside the range of probability." The Wall Street Journal editorialized that stocks were not overvalued and that "the market has not yet caught up with real values."

Such was the confidence—or perhaps the willful blindness—of the era. Those who raised concerns were marginalized, their warnings dismissed as the pessimism of those who simply didn't understand the new economic paradigm America had supposedly entered.

—-

The atmosphere in the final months before the crash had that strange quality we have observed in other pre-crisis periods—a forced optimism covering growing unease. Trading volume began to fluctuate wildly. Market volatility increased. There were several sharp breaks followed by recoveries.

By the summer of 1929, insiders were quietly stepping back. Paul Warburg sold his stocks. Bernard Baruch, one of Wall Street's most successful speculators, began liquidating his positions. Joseph P. Kennedy famously said he knew it was time to get out when his shoeshine boy started giving him stock tips.

Yet publicly, the champagne continued to flow. The rich threw lavish parties. Speakeasies (it was, after all, still Prohibition) did brisk business. F. Scott Fitzgerald captured the era's glittering surface in The Great Gatsby, published in 1925, writing of "the inexhaustible charm that rose and fell in it, the jingle of it, the cymbal's song of it."

On September 3, 1929, the Dow Jones Industrial Average reached its peak of 381.17. Over the next eight weeks, it would lose over 40 percent of its value. On October 24—"Black Thursday"—the market lost 11 percent of its value at the opening bell. Five days later came "Black Tuesday," when the market lost an additional 12 percent amid record trading volume.

By mid-November, the market had lost over $30 billion in value—more than the total cost of World War I to the United States. By 1932, the Dow would bottom out at 41.22—almost 90 percent below its peak.

The champagne bubble had not just popped; it had shattered.

—

What makes the Roaring Twenties so instructive is not just the spectacular nature of the boom and bust, but the psychological patterns that accompanied them. We see the same elements that appeared in the Tulip Mania and the South Sea Bubble, now playing out on a national scale in a modern industrial economy.

First came the narrative of a new era—the belief that traditional economic constraints no longer applied because of technological and social transformation. Radio, automobiles, and electricity weren't just new products; they were seen as fundamentally changing the economic equations.

Then came the democratization of speculation, as ordinary Americans were drawn into the market. What had once been the domain of professionals became a national pastime, with predictable results: amateur investors driven more by emotion than analysis, trading on margin with money they couldn't afford to lose.

Next was the marginalization of skeptics. Those who warned of trouble ahead were not just disagreed with but dismissed as fundamentally failing to understand the new economic reality. The optimists weren't merely hopeful; they were certain.

Finally, there was that strange, electric quality in the air—the sense that something wasn't quite right even as the party continued. The subtle tension between public confidence and private anxiety. The forced quality of the optimism in those final months.

The crash of 1929 did not directly cause the Great Depression that followed. That required a series of policy errors, banking failures, and the collapse of international trade. But the crash revealed the fundamental weaknesses that had been building beneath the surface of prosperity—weaknesses that had been visible all along to those willing to see them.

The lesson of the Roaring Twenties is not that good times must end badly. Rather, it is that prosperity built on imbalance, excessive leverage, and willful blindness to warning signs creates the conditions for its own reversal. The champagne flowed freely in the 1920s, but too few noticed that the foundation beneath the dance floor was beginning to crack.

Chapter 9: 1929: The Day Confidence Died

The morning of October 24, 1929 began like any other autumn Thursday in New York. The air carried that particular crispness that marks the transition from fall to winter. Men in wool suits and fedoras streamed toward Wall Street from subway stations and ferry terminals. Office workers settled at their desks, typists prepared for the day's correspondence. The rhythm of the city—its heartbeat of commerce and ambition—continued its steady pulse.

Yet something was different. Something invisible had shifted.

By 11:00 AM, crowds began to gather outside the New York Stock Exchange. Not the usual mix of messengers and clerks on their morning errands, but a swelling mass of concerned citizens, investors both large and small, and the simply curious. They stood in unusual silence, eyes fixed on the imposing neoclassical building at the corner of Wall and Broad Streets. Inside, a storm was brewing.

The ticker tape—that thin ribbon of paper that connected the trading floor to the outside world—began to fall behind. First by minutes, then by hours. The mechanical marvel that had faithfully reported each transaction could not keep pace with the avalanche of sell orders flooding the exchange. Information, the lifeblood of markets, was failing precisely when it was most needed.

What happened that day, and in the days that followed, was not merely a market correction or even a crash. It was something more profound: the collective death of confidence itself.

—-

In the preceding months, there had been warnings. Roger Babson, an eccentric but respected economist, had predicted a "terrific crash" was coming. The Federal Reserve had raised interest rates, concerned about speculative excess. Financial publications had begun to question the sustainability of stock valuations that had become untethered from corporate earnings.

But these voices were drowned out by the chorus of optimism. Irving Fisher, Yale's eminent economist, had declared just days before that stock prices had reached "a permanently high plateau." The public had embraced a narrative of perpetual prosperity, believing that America had entered a new economic era where the business cycle had been tamed.

This narrative was reinforced by cultural touchstones. F. Scott Fitzgerald's novels captured the zeitgeist of limitless possibility. Advertisements promised not just products but transformation—a washing machine wasn't just an appliance but a ticket to leisure and status. The movies showed a world of glamour that seemed increasingly within reach for the average American.

Behind this optimism lay a more complex reality. The market had been propelled upward not just by genuine economic growth but by an unprecedented expansion of credit. Brokers' loans—money lent to investors to buy stocks on margin—had grown from $3.5 billion in 1926 to over $8.5 billion by 1929. Investors could purchase stocks with as little as 10% down, borrowing the rest. This leverage amplified gains on the way up but would prove catastrophic on the way down.

When the selling began on October 24, it wasn't immediately clear this day would be different from other recent declines. The market had experienced several sharp but brief corrections throughout 1929. Each time, powerful banking interests had stepped in to stabilize prices, reinforcing the belief that the system was fundamentally sound and would correct itself.

By noon, however, the scale of the selling pressure had become unmistakable. The ticker tape delay grew to nearly two hours, creating an information vacuum filled with rumor and fear. Outside on Wall Street, the crowd swelled. A visitor might have mistaken it for a parade gathering, except for the unusual quiet—a collective holding of breath.

Inside the Morgan Bank at 23 Wall Street, directly across from the Exchange, a meeting was hastily convened. Charles Mitchell of National City Bank (today's Citibank), Albert Wiggin of Chase, and Thomas Lamont of J.P. Morgan gathered to organize a response. These were men accustomed to power, who had stabilized markets before. Their plan was simple but bold: pool resources to buy stocks and signal to the market that its most powerful participants remained confident.

At 1:30 PM, Richard Whitney, vice president of the Exchange and broker for J.P. Morgan, strode onto the trading floor. The atmosphere was near panic—traders shouting, paper strewn across the floor, faces flushed with anxiety. Whitney moved deliberately to the U.S. Steel post and placed an order to buy 10,000 shares at $205, well above the current trading price. He then moved methodically from post to post, placing similar orders for other blue-chip stocks.

The intervention worked—temporarily. The market stabilized and even recovered somewhat by the close. Newspapers the next day carried reassuring headlines. President Hoover issued a statement that "the fundamental business of the country... is on a sound and prosperous basis."

But the reprieve was brief. The following Monday, October 28, selling resumed with even greater intensity. And then came Tuesday, October 29—"Black Tuesday"—when the market lost nearly 12% of its value in a single session. This time, there would be no rescue. The bankers' resources, substantial though they were, could not stem the tide of selling that continued for weeks and months.

—-

What collapsed in those autumn days of 1929 was not just stock prices but something more elusive and essential: collective belief. The crash revealed that much of the market's value had been built not on economic fundamentals but on circular confidence—people believed prices would rise because they believed others believed prices would rise.

When this self-reinforcing cycle reversed, it did so with devastating speed and thoroughness. The market, which had seemed to operate by its own mysterious laws of perpetual growth, suddenly revealed itself as all too human—subject to fear, uncertainty, and the brutal mathematics of leverage unwinding.

By mid-November, the New York Times index of industrial stocks had fallen 47% from its September peak. But this was only the beginning. The decline would continue, with brief rallies offering false hope, until July 1932, when the Dow Jones Industrial Average bottomed at 41.22—nearly 90% below its 1929 high.

The human toll behind these numbers was immense. While tales of ruined investors jumping from windows were largely exaggerated, the psychological devastation was real. Fortunes accumulated over lifetimes vanished in days. Middle-class families who had embraced stock ownership as a path to prosperity saw their savings evaporate. The social contract seemed suddenly, violently broken.

—

Perhaps most significant was how the crash transformed America's relationship with risk and uncertainty. Before October 1929, financial markets had been viewed with a kind of innocent optimism—a mechanism that reliably converted savings into wealth through the miracle of compound growth. After the crash, markets came to be seen as volatile, unpredictable, potentially dangerous systems requiring careful regulation and oversight.

The crash also revealed how financial contagion spreads. What began as a stock market decline quickly infected the broader economy. Banks that had lent money for stock purchases faced defaults.

Consumers, feeling suddenly poorer, cut spending. Businesses, seeing demand fall, reduced production and laid off workers. Each contraction reinforced the others in a downward spiral that would become the Great Depression.

In the stillness that followed the crash, as Americans attempted to make sense of what had happened, a painful truth emerged: confidence, once broken, cannot be quickly restored. Trust in institutions, in experts, in the very idea of progress itself had been profoundly shaken. The nation would eventually rebuild its economy and its faith in markets, but never again with the same innocence.

The lessons of 1929 remind us that markets are not merely economic mechanisms but social constructs built on shared beliefs. When those beliefs falter, the consequences extend far beyond balance sheets and bottom lines. They reach into our collective psychology, reshaping how we understand risk, opportunity, and the future itself.

As one Wall Street veteran later reflected: "October 1929 taught me that the three most important words in finance aren't 'margin of safety' or 'buy and hold.' They're 'I don't know.' Markets demand humility, because confidence—even when shared by millions—can evaporate in a single day."

Chapter 10: The New Deal and the Reconstruction of Hope

In the winter of 1933, America stood at the edge of the abyss. The banking system had effectively collapsed. Unemployment had reached 25 percent. Industrial production had fallen to nearly half its pre-crash levels. The stock market had surrendered 90 percent of its value. Farm foreclosures occurred at a rate of twenty thousand per month. In cities across the nation, breadlines stretched for blocks.

This was not merely an economic crisis, but a crisis of faith. The American story—one of progress, opportunity, and the rewards of hard work—had been shattered. The system that many had trusted implicitly now seemed not just flawed but fundamentally broken.

It was into this landscape of despair that Franklin Delano Roosevelt stepped on March 4, 1933. His inauguration came at perhaps the darkest moment of the Depression, just days after a nationwide banking panic had forced every financial institution in the country to close its doors.

"The only thing we have to fear is fear itself," Roosevelt declared in his inaugural address. These words, now embedded in our collective memory, were more than mere rhetoric. They represented a profound understanding of the psychological dimensions of economic collapse. Roosevelt recognized that beyond the material devastation lay a deeper crisis—a collapse of confidence, a failure of nerve, a paralysis of will.

The New Deal that followed was not simply a set of economic policies. It was a deliberate reconstruction of hope.

—-

When we study financial history, we tend to focus on the mechanics of markets—interest rates, fiscal policies, monetary interventions. But what the New Deal teaches us is that economies are also psychological and social systems. They depend on shared beliefs, mutual trust, and collective narratives about the future.

Consider the Banking Act of 1933. Beyond its technical provisions separating commercial and investment banking, it established the Federal Deposit Insurance Corporation. For the first time, ordinary Americans could be certain their savings were protected, not by the promise of an individual bank, but by the full faith and credit of the United States government. This was not just financial engineering—it was the reconstruction of trust.

Or consider the Securities Act of 1933 and the Securities Exchange Act of 1934, which created the Securities and Exchange Commission. These laws did more than impose disclosure requirements and prohibit market manipulation. They reestablished the fundamental premise that markets should be forums for investment rather than gambling halls, that information should be shared rather than hoarded, that the rules should be the same for the powerful and the powerless.

"We are going to make a country," Roosevelt said, "in which no one is left out." This vision animated programs like the Civilian Conservation Corps, which put three million young men to work planting trees, building parks, and constructing roads. It inspired the Works Progress Administration, which employed artists to paint murals, writers to document American life, and laborers to build schools, hospitals, and airports.

These programs were economic in nature, but they served a deeper purpose. They reconnected Americans to a sense of shared purpose and collective possibility. They rebuilt not just infrastructure but the social fabric itself.

—-

The New Deal was not without its critics, then or now. Some argued that it expanded government power beyond constitutional limits.

Others claimed it impeded the natural recovery of markets. Still others believed it did not go far enough in addressing structural inequalities.

These debates continue to shape our political discourse. But what remains beyond dispute is that the New Deal represented a fundamental reimagining of the relationship between government, markets, and citizens. It established a new social contract, one that recognized that unregulated markets could produce not just inequality but catastrophe, and that government had a legitimate role in ensuring basic economic security.

This reimagining did not happen overnight. The New Deal was not a single coherent program but a series of experiments, some successful, others less so. Roosevelt himself acknowledged this improvisational quality: "It is common sense to take a method and try it. If it fails, admit it frankly and try another. But above all, try something."

This willingness to experiment, to adapt, to learn from failure—this too was part of the reconstruction of hope. It suggested that even in the face of unprecedented challenges, human agency remained possible. Problems created by human decisions could be solved by human decisions.

—

By 1936, the worst of the Depression had passed. The economy was growing again. Unemployment, while still high, had been significantly reduced. The banking system was stable. The stock market had regained much of its lost ground.

But the deeper legacy of the New Deal lay in its transformation of American expectations. Social Security established the principle that the elderly should not face destitution. Unemployment insurance recognized that job loss should not mean catastrophe. Labor protections affirmed that workers deserved basic rights and dignities.

These changes represented a profound shift in how Americans thought about economic risk and security. The idea that individuals should bear all economic risks alone, that markets should operate without constraints, that government should remain passive in the face of suffering—these notions, so dominant in the 1920s, had been fundamentally challenged.

This shift did not eliminate economic cycles. It did not prevent future financial crises. But it created a framework of institutions, regulations, and social insurance programs that would provide guardrails for the economy and safety nets for citizens.

—

The story of the New Deal offers us lessons that transcend its historical moment. It reminds us that economic systems are not natural phenomena but human creations that can be redesigned when they fail. It teaches us that confidence, once shattered, must be deliberately reconstructed through both practical actions and compelling narratives. It suggests that hope is not merely an emotional state but a social resource that can be cultivated through collective action.

Perhaps most importantly, it demonstrates that the calm after the storm does not arrive by itself. It must be built, patiently and deliberately, through institutions that embody our highest values and policies that translate those values into everyday realities.

As we navigate our own economic uncertainties—our asset bubbles and banking crises, our technological disruptions and growing inequalities—we would do well to remember this lesson. The reconstruction of hope is never merely technical. It requires us to ask fundamental questions about what kind of economy we want, what risks we are willing to share, what responsibilities we owe to one another.

These questions are not just economic. They are moral and political. They concern not just how markets function but how society functions. They invite us to consider not just the efficiency of our economic arrangements but their fairness, not just their productivity but their purpose.

The New Deal, for all its flaws and limitations, represented one society's attempt to answer these questions in the aftermath of catastrophe. The answers we find may be different. But the questions remain the same.

Chapter 11: The Dot-Com Dream

In the late afternoon of December 9, 1998, a thirty-five-year-old financial analyst named Henry Blodget made a prediction that would come to symbolize an era. Speaking with quiet confidence to a CNBC reporter, he suggested that Amazon—then trading at $242 per share—would reach $400 within twelve months. The stock hit that target just three weeks later.

This was not simply a lucky guess about a single company. It was a moment that crystallized the spirit of a time—a period when the future seemed to be rushing toward us with unprecedented speed, carrying limitless possibility in its wake.

—-

The 1990s dawned in the shadow of the Cold War's end. As the Berlin Wall fell and the Soviet Union dissolved, a peculiar optimism took hold in Western economies. History, some suggested, had reached its end point with the triumph of liberal democracy and free-market capitalism. The future had arrived, and it wore an American face.

Into this moment of geopolitical confidence came a technological revolution that promised to transform human connection itself. The internet—previously the domain of government researchers, academics, and technological enthusiasts—was becoming accessible to ordinary people. What had been a specialized communication network was evolving into something more profound: a new dimension of human experience.

The World Wide Web, with its graphical interfaces and hyperlinks, transformed an intimidating technological landscape into something anyone could navigate. Email addresses began appearing on business cards. Terms like "surfing" and "online" entered the common vocabulary. By mid-decade, the digital frontier had been opened for settlement.

"The internet fundamentally changes the rules," became the mantra of the era. It was repeated in boardrooms and venture capital firms, in university computer labs and suburban garages. Distance would no longer matter. Information would flow freely. Middlemen would disappear. Everything would be disrupted.

This was not merely technological enthusiasm. It was a comprehensive economic philosophy—one that promised unlimited growth without the constraints of traditional business cycles. The old metrics—profits, cash flow, price-to-earnings ratios—were declared obsolete. What mattered now was "eyeballs," "mindshare," and "first-mover advantage."

—-

Silicon Valley had always maintained a certain distance from Wall Street, both geographically and philosophically. The engineers and programmers who built the digital revolution often viewed themselves as creating something more meaningful than mere profit. They were building the future—a noble calling that transcended ordinary commerce.

But as the decade progressed, these worlds began to merge. The Netscape IPO in August 1995 marked a turning point. Here was a company with minimal revenue and no profits, yet investors valued it at $2.9 billion by the end of its first trading day. The company's 24-year-old co-founder, Marc Andreessen, appeared on the cover of Time magazine, barefoot and seated on a throne—the new royalty of the digital age.

Wall Street, which had initially regarded technology companies with skepticism, began to embrace the sector with growing enthusiasm. Investment banks competed fiercely to underwrite technology IPOs. Venture capital, once a relatively modest corner of the financial world, expanded dramatically. Between 1995 and 2000, venture investment in the United States grew from $8 billion to $100 billion annually.

The language of finance and technology blended into a new dialect. Companies no longer "went public"—they had "liquidity events." They weren't valued on earnings but on "burn rates" and "customer acquisition costs." The future wasn't years away; it was quarters. And in this accelerated timeframe, traditional caution seemed like a liability rather than a virtue.

—-

By 1999, the dream had taken full form. Internet stocks had become the modern equivalent of Dutch tulip bulbs—objects of desire whose value seemed to have no natural ceiling. The NASDAQ Composite, heavily weighted with technology companies, rose 86 percent that year alone. Companies added ".com" to their names and watched their stock prices soar. Pets.com, with its sock puppet mascot, became a cultural phenomenon despite having no clear path to profitability.

The most striking aspect of this period was not the financial exuberance—bubbles have occurred throughout economic history—but the sincere belief that we were witnessing a fundamental transformation of human society. This was not just about money. It was about a new world being born.

"We're creating an architecture for the future," said one prominent venture capitalist at the time. "The old economy is dead," declared the cover of Wired magazine. "Resistance is futile," warned countless conference speakers and business consultants.

Those who questioned the valuations or business models of internet companies were not simply viewed as skeptical investors. They were cast as enemies of progress itself—modern-day Luddites who failed to grasp the magnitude of the transformation underway. The criticism that most stung these doubters was not that they were wrong about financial projections, but that they "didn't get it."

—-

And yet, beneath the surface optimism, subtle warning signs appeared. The average internet company that went public in 1999 had lost $12 million in the prior year on revenue of just $17 million. Traditional metrics suggested many of these businesses were fundamentally unsound, but such concerns were dismissed as applying "old world" thinking to "new economy" companies.

Alan Greenspan, then Chairman of the Federal Reserve, gave a speech in December 1996 questioning whether the market might be experiencing "irrational exuberance." The market briefly dipped, then continued its ascent with even greater momentum. By 1999, Greenspan had largely abandoned his skepticism, suggesting that perhaps technology truly had changed the fundamental equations of economic value.

Warren Buffett, the legendary value investor, was openly mocked for refusing to invest in technology companies. At Berkshire Hathaway's annual meeting in 1999, shareholders questioned whether he had lost his touch. "I don't know how to value these companies," Buffett admitted. His honesty was interpreted as confession of irrelevance.

A peculiar inversion had occurred: caution had become the risky position. Those who remained on the sidelines watched colleagues, friends, and neighbors accumulate paper fortunes. The fear of missing out—what would later be abbreviated as "FOMO"—became a powerful psychological force driving further investment, further speculation, further belief.

—-

Like all bubbles, the dot-com era created its own reality distortion field. Within this field, the normal rules of business and economics appeared temporarily suspended. Companies spent lavishly on Super

Bowl advertisements, elaborate office spaces, and employee perks. Twenty-something CEOs appeared on magazine covers. Private jets shuttled executives between Silicon Valley and New York financial institutions eager to fund the next big thing.

The language of revolution permeated everything. "We don't have time for traditional business plans," explained one startup founder. "We're moving at internet speed." The implication was clear: those who took time to think, to plan, to question, would be left behind.

This was the peculiar stillness before the storm—not a calm stillness, but the heightened, electric stillness that precedes a thunderclap. It was a moment when the collective belief in a narrative became so powerful that it briefly reshaped reality itself.

In March 2000, the NASDAQ reached its peak of 5,048.62. From there, it would fall 78% over the next two and a half years. More than $5 trillion in market value would evaporate. Thousands of companies would disappear. The dream would end.

But in the moment—in that strange, suspended time when the future seemed both utterly certain and infinitely malleable—few could imagine the coming collapse. The warning signs were there, visible to those willing to see them. But the dream was too compelling, too aligned with our deepest hopes about technology and progress, to be easily abandoned.

The dot-com bubble, like all financial manias, revealed something essential about human nature: our capacity to transform hope into conviction, to mistake narrative for reality, to believe collectively in possibilities that, in retrospect, defy basic economic logic.

It also revealed something about the particular moment in history—the end of one millennium and the beginning of another—when technology promised to free us from the constraints of the physical world. The internet truly was revolutionary. The mistake was not in recognizing its transformative potential, but in assuming that transformation would follow a straight line upward, enriching everyone who claimed a stake in the future.

In the quiet moments before the market opened each morning, some investors must have felt a flicker of doubt, a momentary questioning of the collective narrative. But these doubts were easily pushed aside in the rush of a new trading day, in the excitement of another IPO announcement, in the shared conviction that this time truly was different.

It was a dream from which America would eventually awaken. But while it lasted, it felt more real than reality itself.

Chapter 12: The Day Traders of 1999

On an ordinary Tuesday morning in 1999, Mark Barton walked into All-Tech Investment Group in Atlanta carrying a paper bag. Inside were two loaded pistols. By the time his rampage across two brokerage firms ended, nine people were dead. When police searched Barton's home, they found a note: "I don't plan to live very much longer, just long enough to kill as many of the people that greedily sought my destruction."

What investigators discovered next revealed a darker story beneath the tragedy. Barton had lost over $500,000 day trading in the volatile markets of the late 1990s. His personal financial collapse had occurred during what appeared to be the greatest wealth-creation opportunity in a generation.

This is not a chapter about violence. It is about the particular fever that gripped America in the final months of the twentieth century—a fever that transformed ordinary people into market speculators, and that reveals something essential about the psychological atmosphere that precedes economic turning points.

—-

The phenomenon of day trading—buying and selling stocks within the same trading session—was not new to Wall Street. Professional floor traders had engaged in this practice for generations. What changed in the late 1990s was accessibility. Suddenly, anyone with a computer, an internet connection, and a few thousand dollars could participate in what had previously been an exclusive domain.

By 1999, an estimated seven million Americans had become online traders. Most were not day traders in the strict sense, but a significant minority—perhaps 250,000 people—had quit their jobs to trade full-time. They gathered in specialized "day trading shops," renting desk space and computer terminals for hundreds of dollars per day, plus commissions on every trade.

"I was making more in a day than I made in a month as an accountant," recalled Jonathan Miller, a former day trader I interviewed for this book. "You'd walk into these trading rooms and feel the electricity. Everyone watching multiple screens, making split-second decisions. It felt like being in a casino where everyone had figured out how to beat the house."

The technological infrastructure that made this possible had emerged rapidly. In 1996, online brokerage accounts were rare. By 1999, they were commonplace. Commissions that had once cost hundreds of dollars per trade fell to $8 at discount brokers like E*Trade and Ameritrade. The Securities and Exchange Commission's order handling rules, implemented in 1997, allowed electronic communication networks (ECNs) to compete with traditional market makers, narrowing spreads and creating new opportunities for quick profits.

The day traders of 1999 were not simply gambling. They had developed a distinctive culture, complete with its own language, heroes, and mythology. They spoke of "scalping" (capturing tiny price movements), "fading" (betting against price momentum), and "SOES bandits" (traders who used the Small Order Execution System to pick off slow-moving market makers).

They read books like "Electronic Day Traders' Secrets" and subscribed to real-time data services that cost hundreds of dollars monthly. They gathered on message boards like Raging Bull and Silicon Investor, sharing tips and trading strategies. And they told themselves a compelling story: that they were market revolutionaries, using technology to level the playing field against Wall Street's elite.

—-

What made this moment unique was not just the technology but the backdrop against which it occurred. The stock market had been rising steadily since 1995. By 1999, the NASDAQ had tripled in just three years. A new vocabulary had emerged to justify stratospheric valuations for companies with no earnings: "mindshare," "eyeballs," "stickiness." Traditional metrics like price-to-earnings ratios seemed obsolete.

In this environment, day traders developed strategies that would have been suicidal in normal markets but worked brilliantly in the bubble. The most common was simply to buy whatever was moving upward and ride the momentum.

"The strategy was embarrassingly simple," said Miller. "Find a stock that was up 10% pre-market, buy it at the open, and sell when it was up another 5%. It worked almost every time. When it didn't, you'd just hold until it came back—which it always did, until suddenly it didn't."

Another popular approach was to trade on pure news flow, regardless of fundamentals. When a company announced anything remotely connected to the internet—even something as simple as launching a website—its stock would often double or triple in a single day.

Perhaps the most revealing strategy was what traders called "buying the bubble." This involved purchasing stocks that had already risen dramatically, on the theory that irrational exuberance would drive them even higher.

"We knew it was a bubble," one former day trader told me. "We just thought we were smart enough to get out before it popped."

—

The media both chronicled and amplified the phenomenon. CNBC, which had launched in 1989, became the soundtrack of the bubble. Programs like "Power Lunch" and "Street Signs" turned market analysts into celebrities. The network's viewership increased 242% between 1997 and early 2000.

Financial news websites proliferated. TheStreet.com, founded by hedge fund manager Jim Cramer, went public in May 1999 at $19 per share and hit $60 on its first day of trading. MarketWatch, CBS.Marketwatch, and dozens of similar sites competed to provide real-time information to the growing army of amateur traders.

Books promising to reveal the secrets of day trading became bestsellers. "Electronic Day Trading to Win" by Bob Baird and Craig McBurney instructed readers: "Don't think of this as investing. This is a business, and the product is money."

The cultural message was clear: Trading was no longer the province of the elite. It was a democratic opportunity, a new American frontier where ordinary people could strike it rich through quick thinking and technological savvy.

—-

What's striking in retrospect is how the day trading phenomenon mirrored broader societal shifts. The 1990s had seen the rise of a new individualism. Traditional institutions—corporations, government, unions—seemed increasingly irrelevant in an age of technological empowerment. The day trader embodied this ethos: self-reliant, tech-savvy, unburdened by convention.

This was also the era of "The New Economy," when traditional economic constraints supposedly no longer applied. Day traders, with their disregard for fundamental analysis, were the perfect market participants for this narrative. They traded on momentum, sentiment, and narrative rather than earnings or cash flow.

The psychological atmosphere in day trading shops by late 1999 was one of barely contained mania. Traders would cheer when stocks moved in their favor, high-fiving neighbors and shouting across the room. When someone hit a particularly large gain, it wasn't uncommon for the entire room to go out for an impromptu celebration.

"There was this sense that we'd discovered a secret," recalled Miller. "We were making more money than doctors or lawyers, and all we needed was a computer and some courage. In retrospect, it was mass delusion, but at the time, it felt like clarity."

—-

Not everyone was swept up in the euphoria. The Securities and Exchange Commission issued warnings about the risks of day trading. A study by the North American Securities Administrators Association in 1999 concluded that "70 percent of public traders will not only lose, but will almost certainly lose everything they invest."

These warnings were largely ignored. When confronted with statistics showing that most day traders lost money, the typical response was that those failures simply lacked the right temperament or strategy. It was a perfect example of what psychologists call "attribution bias"—attributing others' failures to personal flaws while seeing one's own successes as the result of skill.

The reality, which became painfully clear after the bubble burst, was that day trading profits in 1999 were not primarily the result of skill. They were the product of a directional market with unprecedented momentum. Everyone looked like a genius in a market that rose 85% in a single year.

—-

By December 1999, the day trading phenomenon had reached its apotheosis. Trading volumes on the NASDAQ hit record highs. Discount brokers were opening hundreds of thousands of new accounts monthly. The NASDAQ would peak three months later at 5,048.62, more than double its level from just a year earlier.

What's remarkable in hindsight is how clearly the day trading boom signaled the market top. When taxi drivers, teachers, and retirees abandon their professions to speculate full-time, it suggests a market running out of new participants. When trading itself, rather than underlying business value, becomes the primary focus, the market has detached from economic reality.

The aftermath was predictable yet somehow unexpected. As the market began to fall in spring 2000, day traders initially saw it as an opportunity. They had been trained in a bull market to "buy the dip"—to view any decline as temporary. This strategy, which had worked flawlessly for years, suddenly failed catastrophically.

By the end of 2000, most day trading shops had closed. The survivors limped along for another year before shuttering. Individual traders who had quit their jobs to trade full-time returned to conventional employment, if they could find it. Many had lost not just their trading capital but their life savings, home equity, even their retirement accounts.

—-

What can we learn from the day traders of 1999?

First, they remind us that financial manias are not simply about assets—they're about identity. People didn't just invest in internet stocks; they became "day traders." This transformation of financial activity into personal identity makes it extraordinarily difficult to maintain objectivity.

Second, the episode reveals how quickly new norms can establish themselves. Within just a few years, behavior that would have seemed reckless became conventional wisdom. When everyone around you is making money through speculation, prudence starts to look like foolishness.

Third, and perhaps most importantly, the day trading phenomenon demonstrates how the final stages of a bubble can create their own temporary reality. For a brief moment, the day traders' worldview was correct. Markets did move on momentum rather than fundamentals.

Stocks did go up simply because they had gone up before. Technical analysis did outperform careful study of business models.

This temporary confirmation creates a powerful illusion of mastery. It suggests that the participants have discovered something essential about how markets work. Only later does it become clear that what they discovered was merely how markets behave during bubbles.

—-

I sometimes wonder what happened to all those day traders. Most disappeared quietly, their dreams of market riches replaced by the mundane reality of regular employment. Some found their way into other financial roles, chastened but wiser. A few, those who recognized early that the game had changed, preserved their capital and their careers.

And a tiny minority—those who understood that they were surfing a wave of irrational exuberance rather than demonstrating investment skill—managed to extract themselves before the collapse. They are the survivors who remind us that even in moments of collective delusion, individual clarity remains possible.

The day traders of 1999 weren't fools. They were ordinary people caught up in extraordinary times. Their story is not one of personal failing but of collective psychology—of how markets can create environments that temporarily reward behavior that, in the long run, leads to ruin.

As we examine other moments of market euphoria, remember the day traders hunched over their screens, convinced they had discovered the secret to wealth. Their experience teaches us something profound: In finance, as in weather, the most dangerous moment often comes when the sky seems clearest.

Chapter 13: The Slow Swell of the Housing Bubble

Unlike the frenzied pace of the dot-com bubble, which rocketed upward and burst with spectacular speed, the housing bubble that defined the first decade of the 2000s rose with a deceptive gentleness. It was a tide rather than a wave—advancing so gradually that most standing on the shore hardly noticed the water rising around their ankles, then their knees, until they found themselves suddenly submerged.

The origins of this slow swell can be traced to the wreckage of the previous crisis. As tech stocks crumbled in 2000 and 2001, the Federal Reserve, led by Alan Greenspan, slashed interest rates from 6.5% to 1% to cushion the economic impact. This unprecedented monetary intervention would have far-reaching consequences that few anticipated. Money, suddenly cheap and abundant, began seeking new vessels.

Real estate seemed the perfect harbor—tangible, comprehensible, and historically stable. Unlike the abstract promises of internet companies, houses were physical assets you could touch, live in, improve. They represented the American dream made manifest in wood, brick, and drywall.

"The nice thing about houses," one mortgage broker told me years later, "is that everyone understands them. My clients couldn't explain a price-to-earnings ratio, but they knew what a three-bedroom colonial was worth in their neighborhood."

This fundamental familiarity created a dangerous comfort. If the dot-com bubble had been fueled by the exotic and unfamiliar, the housing bubble drew strength from the opposite—the deeply familiar transformed into something new.

By 2003, the narrative had begun to take shape. Housing prices in coastal cities had been rising steadily, but not yet at rates that seemed historically anomalous. What changed was the story Americans began telling themselves about what these increases meant.

A subtle shift occurred in how people viewed their homes—from places to live to investment vehicles. "Your home is your ATM" became a common refrain on financial television. Homeowners were encouraged to tap their growing equity through refinancing and home equity loans, using their houses not just as shelter but as sources of consumable wealth.

The psychological transformation was profound. Housing had always been considered a solid but unspectacular investment that approximately kept pace with inflation. Now, suddenly, it was seen as a can't-miss opportunity for wealth creation.

"I remember sitting at a neighborhood barbecue in Phoenix in 2004," a retired schoolteacher told me. "Everyone was talking about their home values the way people used to discuss their children's accomplishments. The couple across from me had made more on their house in the past year than I had earned teaching high school English."

This shift coincided with an explosion of financial innovation in mortgage lending. The old model—where a local bank issued a mortgage, held it on their books, and had every incentive to ensure the borrower could repay—gave way to a complex chain of securitization. Mortgages were originated, then sold, packaged into securities, sliced into tranches, and distributed globally.

This severed the relationship between risk and responsibility. The originator of a loan no longer needed to worry about its quality, only whether it could be sold up the chain. The result was predictable: lending standards deteriorated as mortgage products proliferated.

—-

The financial industry invented products with names that sounded reassuringly technical: interest-only loans, negative amortization mortgages, stated-income loans (mockingly called "liar loans" by industry insiders), and adjustable-rate mortgages with teaser rates. Each innovation pushed the boundaries of what was possible, enabling people to buy homes they could not truly afford.

Unlike the day traders of the dot-com era, who at least knew they were gambling, many homebuyers were unaware of the risks they were assuming. The complexity was often intentional—buried in fine print and technical language.

A mortgage broker in Florida explained to me: "I had clients sign documents they didn't understand, with terms that would reset in ways they couldn't afford. But everyone up the chain was making money, and the client got the house they wanted. The music was playing, and nobody wanted to be the one to stop dancing."

By 2005, the signs of excess were becoming difficult to ignore. In Las Vegas, Phoenix, and parts of Florida and California, home prices were increasing at 20% or more annually. The national homeownership rate reached an all-time high of 69.2%. Television shows like "Flip This House" and "Property Ladder" turned real estate speculation into entertainment.

Yet even as the bubble inflated to historic proportions, a strange calm prevailed in economic policy circles. In 2005, Ben Bernanke, then an economic advisor to President Bush, acknowledged regional "froth" in housing markets but dismissed the possibility of a nationwide housing collapse.

"We've never had a decline in house prices on a nationwide basis," he said, unwittingly highlighting how historical patterns can blind us to emerging risks.

—

The calm extended to regulatory agencies that might have intervened. The Federal Reserve, despite warnings from staff economists about dangerous lending practices, chose not to exercise its authority to regulate mortgage origination. The Office of the Comptroller of the Currency actively blocked state efforts to crack down on predatory lending.

This institutional passivity reflected a deeper philosophical belief that markets would naturally self-correct. The idea that millions of individual decisions could collectively produce a massive mispricing of an entire asset class seemed implausible to many economists trained in efficient market theory.

Meanwhile, on the ground, the bubble created its own reality. As prices rose, lending standards fell. By 2006, nearly half of all mortgages issued were subprime or Alt-A (a category just above subprime). The percentage of mortgages with little or no documentation had risen from virtually zero to nearly 40% of all loans.

The most telling sign of excess came in the form of "NINJA" loans—No Income, No Job, No Assets—which allowed people with no verifiable means of repayment to purchase homes. The absurdity of such products was obscured by their packaging into complex securities that received investment-grade ratings from credit agencies.

"The whole system depended on housing prices continuing to rise," a former ratings agency analyst told me. "It was like a perpetual motion machine—it worked perfectly as long as you didn't ask where the energy was coming from."

—-

By late 2006, the first hairline cracks appeared. Housing prices plateaued in formerly hot markets. The inventory of unsold homes began to grow. Early subprime lenders started to report rising delinquencies.

Yet the broader market remained calm. The Dow Jones Industrial Average continued climbing to new records. Federal Reserve officials maintained that any housing slowdown would be "contained" and wouldn't affect the broader economy.

This period—the plateau before the plunge—is perhaps the most instructive. The mathematics of the situation had become unsustainable: home prices had far outpaced income growth, speculation had replaced fundamental demand, and trillions of dollars of mortgage securities depended on the continued ability of borrowers to refinance or sell at higher prices.

But mathematics alone doesn't move markets. Markets move when psychology shifts, when the collective story changes from one of opportunity to one of risk. That shift happens slowly, then suddenly.

In the quiet months of early 2007, as foreclosures began their inexorable rise and the first mortgage companies filed for bankruptcy, the air grew heavy with that peculiar stillness that precedes a storm. The housing bubble had reached its fullest expansion. The only question was what would provide the pin.

Chapter 14: 2008: The Sound of Breaking Glass

There is a particular quality to the sound of a financial system breaking. It doesn't happen all at once, with a dramatic crash like a window shattered by a thrown stone. Rather, it begins with almost imperceptible cracks—small fissures that spread slowly at first, then with accelerating speed, until what once seemed solid suddenly gives way entirely.

In early 2007, these first cracks appeared in the seemingly impenetrable edifice of American finance. New Century Financial, then the second-largest subprime mortgage lender in the country, announced "unexpected losses." The language was technical, buried in financial statements, but it was the first public admission that something was fundamentally wrong with the mortgage machine that had been running at full capacity for years.

By summer, the cracks had widened. Two Bear Stearns hedge funds that had invested heavily in mortgage-backed securities collapsed. Their names—the "High-Grade Structured Credit Fund" and the "High-Grade Structured Credit Enhanced Leveraged Fund"—would later seem like cruel jokes, their very complexity a warning sign that went unheeded. Still, most financial commentators described these as "contained" problems. The word "contained" would become a dark refrain throughout the crisis, repeated with diminishing conviction as the damage spread.

In the hallways of investment banks, at the Federal Reserve, in the Treasury Department, and in newsrooms, there was a growing sense of unease—that strange stillness that precedes a storm. But publicly, the message remained one of reassurance. In August 2007, Jim Cramer's famous on-air meltdown on CNBC—"They know nothing!"—stood out precisely because it broke the unwritten rule of maintaining calm.

"The subprime market is contained," said Treasury Secretary Henry Paulson in April 2007.

"The impact on the broader economy and financial markets of the problems in the subprime market seems likely to be contained," said Fed Chairman Ben Bernanke in March of that same year.

This was the peculiar quiet before the financial crisis—not an absence of warning signs, but a collective decision to speak of them in hushed tones.

—-

By September 2008, the cracks had become fissures, and the fissures had become chasms. The federal government had already placed mortgage giants Fannie Mae and Freddie Mac into conservatorship—a polite term for what was essentially nationalization. But it was the weekend of September 13-14 that would transform the slow-motion crisis into a full-blown financial panic.

That weekend, federal officials and Wall Street executives gathered at the Federal Reserve Bank of New York for emergency meetings to determine the fate of Lehman Brothers, the 158-year-old investment bank that was rapidly running out of cash. The air in those wood-paneled rooms was thick with tension, sleep-deprived bankers and regulators working through the night to find a solution.

Unlike Bear Stearns months earlier, no rescue materialized for Lehman. By Sunday night, it was clear the firm would file for bankruptcy—the largest in American history.

"We did not have the authority to save Lehman," Treasury Secretary Paulson would later insist. Whether this was strictly true remains debated by economists and historians. What is certain is that the decision not to rescue Lehman was partly a moral judgment—a response to the public outrage over earlier bailouts, a desire to combat "moral hazard" by letting at least one major firm face the consequences of its actions.

It was a principled stand that the financial system could not bear.

—

The morning of Monday, September 15, 2008, dawned with news that Lehman Brothers was bankrupt. The Dow Jones Industrial Average fell 504 points that day—a severe but not unprecedented drop. What made this moment different was not what happened in the visible stock market, but in the invisible plumbing of the financial system.

The commercial paper market—where corporations borrow short-term money to fund their daily operations—seized up. The money market funds—where ordinary Americans parked cash they considered as safe as bank deposits—began to "break the buck," falling below the sacrosanct $1 per share value that was their foundational promise. The interbank lending market—where financial institutions lend to each other overnight—effectively shut down as trust evaporated.

It was as if all the oxygen had suddenly been sucked out of the financial ecosystem.

"In the span of a few weeks, many of our nation's largest financial institutions failed or were forced to merge to avoid insolvency," Bernanke would later testify. "Capital markets froze, and credit stopped flowing to businesses and families."

The sound of this breaking was not a crash but a sudden, eerie silence—the absence of the normal hum of financial transactions that power modern economies.

—

What made the crisis of 2008 so profound was not just its severity but its comprehensive nature. It wasn't merely a stock market crash or a banking crisis—it was a systemic failure that revealed the deep interconnections that had been built into the global financial architecture.

The mortgage-backed securities and collateralized debt obligations that Wall Street had engineered were supposed to distribute risk. Instead, they had obscured it. Financial institutions had become so entangled that the failure of one threatened the survival of all—a fact that regulators and executives alike had failed to appreciate until it was too late.

The aftermath unfolded with brutal speed. Merrill Lynch, fearing it would be next, sold itself to Bank of America in a hastily arranged weekend deal. AIG, the insurance giant that had written trillions in credit default swaps—essentially insurance on mortgage securities—received an $85 billion government bailout to prevent its collapse from triggering a global financial apocalypse.

Within days, the remaining major investment banks—Goldman Sachs and Morgan Stanley—converted themselves into bank holding companies, ending the era of independent investment banking in America and subjecting themselves to greater regulation in exchange for access to the Federal Reserve's discount window.

By the end of September, Washington Mutual had failed—the largest bank failure in American history. In October, Congress passed the $700 billion Troubled Asset Relief Program (TARP) after an initial rejection sent markets plunging further.

The breaking glass of 2008 was not just the sound of financial institutions failing. It was the shattering of assumptions and beliefs that had guided economic policy for decades.

—-

What makes financial crises distinct from natural disasters is the element of human agency—both in their creation and in their resolution. The crisis of 2008 was not an earthquake or hurricane that struck without warning. It was the culmination of human decisions, policies, incentives, and beliefs that had built up over years.

The breaking glass of 2008 revealed that the financial system had been constructed on a foundation of interconnected illusions:

The illusion that housing prices would always rise.

The illusion that financial innovation had successfully engineered risk away.

The illusion that markets would always self-correct before catastrophic failure.

The illusion that regulators understood the system they were overseeing.

When these illusions shattered simultaneously, they took with them something even more fundamental: trust. Trust in institutions, in experts, in the system itself. The social contract between financial elites and ordinary citizens was revealed to be profoundly one-sided. Wall Street firms that had privatized gains for years now socialized their losses, while millions of Americans lost homes, jobs, and savings.

"It's not fair," became a common refrain—not just from left-wing protesters but from conservative retirees watching their 401(k)s evaporate while the architects of the crisis received government support.

This broken trust would have consequences far beyond economics. The crisis of 2008 didn't just reshape financial markets; it reshaped politics, culture, and social attitudes in ways that continue to reverberate today. The populist movements of the 2010s—on both the left and right—can trace much of their energy back to the moment when the financial system broke and ordinary people were left to pick up the pieces.

—

By the time the dust settled, the American economy had lost nearly 9 million jobs. Unemployment reached 10 percent. Almost $16 trillion in household wealth had vanished. The federal government had committed trillions in guarantees, loans, and outright bailouts.

The human cost was incalculable. Behind the statistics were families who lost homes they had worked decades to secure, workers in their 50s who would never find equivalent employment again, young graduates entering a decimated job market, small business owners watching their life's work disintegrate.

And yet, devastating as it was, the Great Recession was not the Great Depression. The financial system, despite coming to the edge of the abyss, did not collapse entirely. The unemployment rate, while painfully high, peaked at less than half the level reached in the 1930s. The social safety net, though strained, prevented the kind of widespread destitution seen during the Depression.

This was both the success and the failure of the policy response. The emergency interventions—the bailouts, the Federal Reserve's unprecedented monetary policies, the fiscal stimulus—prevented complete collapse. But they also preserved much of the system that had failed, creating a recovery that would be uneven, prolonged, and deeply unsatisfying to many Americans.

The sound of breaking glass in 2008 marked the end of one economic era and the uncertain beginning of another. It was a moment when history did not exactly repeat itself—the lessons of the Great Depression had been learned well enough to prevent its recurrence—but it certainly rhymed.

In the silence that followed the crash, as policymakers worked to rebuild the financial system and restart economic growth, few paused to consider whether they were laying the groundwork for the next crisis even as they cleared away the debris from the last. The emergency measures taken—particularly the unprecedented monetary policies—would themselves become the foundation for new forms of speculation, new asset bubbles, and new vulnerabilities that would only become apparent years later.

The calm that eventually returned was not the stable equilibrium of a system in balance, but the strange stillness that comes before the next storm.

Chapter 15: The Age of Quantitative Easing

In the quiet aftermath of catastrophe, central bankers gathered in wood-paneled rooms to contemplate the unthinkable. The conventional tools of monetary policy—the careful adjustment of interest rates to cool or stimulate economic activity—had reached their limit. By December 2008, the Federal Reserve had lowered its benchmark rate to effectively zero. The economy continued to bleed jobs. Credit markets remained frozen. The patient was not responding to traditional medicine.

What followed was one of the most extraordinary economic experiments in modern history.

"The problem with quantitative easing," Ben Bernanke would later joke, "is that it works in practice, but not in theory." The quip revealed something profound about the moment: we had entered uncharted waters where even the navigators were unsure of the currents.

Quantitative easing—QE, as it came to be known—represented a fundamental shift in how central banks approached economic crisis. Rather than simply adjusting the price of money through interest rates, the Federal Reserve would now directly increase its quantity by purchasing massive amounts of government bonds and mortgage-backed securities. The balance sheet of the Fed, which had hovered around $800 billion before the crisis, would swell to $4.5 trillion by 2015.

The mechanics were complex, but the intent was straightforward: flood the financial system with liquidity, drive down long-term interest rates, and encourage investors to move into riskier assets that might stimulate economic growth. It was monetary policy operating at an entirely new scale.

The first rounds of QE were met with apocalyptic predictions. Critics warned of imminent hyperinflation, the collapse of the dollar, and the destruction of America's financial credibility. Gold prices soared as investors sought shelter from the coming monetary storm. Newspaper headlines questioned whether the Fed had crossed a Rubicon from which there was no return.

The inflation never came. The dollar did not collapse. Instead, something more subtle occurred: asset prices began to rise—first tentatively, then dramatically. The stock market, which had lost more than half its value, began a steady climb that would become the longest bull market in American history. Housing prices eventually stabilized. Corporate bond yields fell to historic lows.

For those with assets—stocks, real estate, financial investments—the recovery was robust. For those without, it was barely perceptible.

"QE created a bifurcated economy," explained former Treasury economist Karen Dynan in 2014. "We engineered a recovery in asset prices that preceded—and in many ways outpaced—the recovery in the real economy."

This divergence between Wall Street and Main Street would have profound social and political consequences in the years to come. The tools that saved the financial system simultaneously widened the very inequalities that had made it fragile.

—-

By 2010, a strange calm had settled over financial markets. Volatility indexes dropped to pre-crisis levels. Interest rates remained at historic lows. Corporate profits recovered while wages stagnated. A new normal emerged—one characterized by abundant liquidity, suppressed volatility, and the persistent sense that central banks would intervene to prevent significant market declines.

The term "Fed put" entered the financial lexicon—the implicit guarantee that the central bank would support asset prices in times of stress. This perception fundamentally altered the psychology of risk. If downside was limited by central bank intervention, why not take greater risks? If cheap money was abundant, why not use more leverage?

Janet Yellen, who succeeded Bernanke as Fed chair in 2014, acknowledged the dilemma. "We are mindful of the potential for financial excesses," she testified to Congress. "But we must balance those concerns against the more immediate risks of a fragile recovery."

The balance was delicate, and the stakes were enormous. The trauma of 2008 remained fresh in institutional memory. No one wanted to risk another financial collapse by withdrawing support too quickly.

—

Meanwhile, something profound was happening to the concept of money itself. As central banks created trillions of dollars, euros, and yen through keystrokes on computers, the nature of currency as a scarce resource seemed increasingly abstract. Money appeared less like a finite commodity and more like a social technology that could be expanded or contracted at will.

This shift in perception coincided with historically low interest rates that persisted not for months, but for years. When money costs nothing to borrow, its value becomes difficult to assess. Traditional models for valuing assets—based on discounting future cash flows—began to break down when the discount rate approached zero.

"We're seeing a fundamental repricing of all assets," noted economist Mohamed El-Erian in 2016. "The anchors we've used for decades are drifting."

In this environment, speculative assets flourished. Venture capital flowed to startups with negative cash flows but compelling narratives.

Private equity firms borrowed cheaply to acquire companies at ever-higher multiples. Real estate in global cities became repositories of wealth rather than simply places to live.

The age of quantitative easing did not create a traditional inflationary spiral in consumer goods. Instead, it created asset inflation—a steady rise in the price of financial assets, real estate, art, collectibles, and other stores of value. This was inflation that did not appear in the consumer price index but was nonetheless real and consequential.

—

By 2017, central banks around the world owned approximately $15 trillion in assets—a figure larger than the entire economy of China. The experiment had moved from emergency measure to seemingly permanent feature of the financial landscape. The question that haunted policy discussions was no longer whether quantitative easing worked, but how it could ever be unwound.

When the Federal Reserve began tentatively raising interest rates and reducing its balance sheet in 2018, markets reacted with volatility that prompted a swift reversal. The lesson seemed clear: the financial system had become dependent on extraordinary monetary support. Removing that support would be neither simple nor painless.

Then came the pandemic of 2020, and central banks responded with quantitative easing on an even larger scale than in 2008. The Fed's balance sheet, which had been gradually reduced to $3.8 trillion, exploded to $7 trillion in a matter of months. The European Central Bank and Bank of Japan followed similar trajectories.

—

What are we to make of this extraordinary period in economic history? The age of quantitative easing represented both triumph and warning.

It prevented the Great Recession from becoming another Great Depression—an achievement that should not be minimized. Yet it also revealed the fragility of a financial system that requires ever-larger interventions to maintain stability.

Perhaps most importantly, it demonstrated how monetary policy, once considered a technical matter best left to experts, had become central to questions of social equity and political legitimacy. The distribution of gains from QE—heavily skewed toward those who already held assets—contributed to populist movements on both left and right. The perception that the system was rigged in favor of financial elites became widespread.

As one anonymous Fed official confided in 2019: "We saved the system, but at the cost of its legitimacy in the eyes of many citizens. That's a price we're still calculating."

The age of quantitative easing represented a strange interregnum—a period between crises when money lost its traditional constraints, when asset prices detached from economic fundamentals, and when the very concept of value became increasingly subjective. It was a calm unlike any other, not because it lacked tension, but because the tension was hidden beneath unprecedented monetary intervention.

Like all periods of artificial stability, it contained within it the seeds of future instability. The patterns were familiar—the suppression of volatility, the reach for yield, the growing comfort with leverage, the collective belief that negative outcomes had been engineered away. These were the same psychological patterns that preceded previous financial crises, now playing out on an even larger scale.

The question was not whether this new equilibrium would eventually break, but how, when, and with what consequences. The calm, as always, preceded the storm.

Chapter 16: Bitcoin and the New Believers

On October 31, 2008, as the global financial system trembled in the aftermath of Lehman Brothers' collapse, an anonymous figure using the pseudonym Satoshi Nakamoto published a nine-page white paper to a cryptography mailing list. The timing was not coincidental. The document, titled "Bitcoin: A Peer-to-Peer Electronic Cash System," proposed a solution to a problem many hadn't yet fully articulated: What if we could no longer trust the institutions that managed our money?

While central banks were preparing to flood the financial system with unprecedented liquidity, Satoshi was proposing something different—a currency with a mathematically fixed supply, immune to the whims of governments and central bankers. The first line of code in Bitcoin's genesis block contained an embedded message: "The Times 03/Jan/2009 Chancellor on brink of second bailout for banks." It wasn't just a timestamp; it was a manifesto.

For years, Bitcoin remained in the shadows, a curiosity traded among cryptographers, libertarians, and tech enthusiasts. A single bitcoin was worth pennies, then dollars. In those early days, one programmer infamously spent 10,000 bitcoins to purchase two pizzas—a transaction that would later be worth hundreds of millions of dollars. But something more profound than price speculation was happening: a new belief system was forming.

—-

The financial crisis of 2008 had fractured trust in traditional financial institutions. Young people who had watched their parents lose homes, retirement savings, and jobs harbored a deep skepticism toward Wall

Street and Washington alike. This disillusionment created fertile ground for alternative narratives about money itself.

"Bitcoin offered something powerful—a story about money that didn't require trusting human institutions," explained Alyson Chen, a sociologist who studies financial subcultures. "Instead, you could trust math, code, and distributed consensus. For a generation that had seen trust in institutions collapse, this was incredibly appealing."

Bitcoin's early adopters weren't just investing in a speculative asset; they were participating in what felt like a revolution. The community developed its own vocabulary, rituals, and moral frameworks. "HODLing"—a misspelling of "holding" from a frantic forum post—became a virtue, signifying unwavering commitment through market volatility. "Nocoiners" were the unenlightened who failed to see the future. Early adopters spoke of being "orange-pilled," a reference to seeing the truth behind the financial system's façade.

The narrative evolved beyond the original libertarian roots. For some, Bitcoin represented a check against government surveillance and control. For others, it was a solution to currency debasement in countries experiencing hyperinflation. For still others, it was simply a technological marvel—the first digital object that couldn't be infinitely copied.

—-

By 2017, what had begun as a fringe experiment had captured mainstream attention. The price of a single bitcoin approached $20,000. CNBC featured hourly price updates. Taxi drivers and hairdressers offered investment advice. Celebrities promoted "initial coin offerings" for new cryptocurrencies, many of which had little purpose beyond speculation.

The atmosphere was electric with possibility. Twenty-three-year-old crypto millionaires purchased Lamborghinis as status symbols. Conferences became revival meetings where speakers proclaimed a new financial order. The language shifted from technical discussions about blockchain architecture to grand visions of societal transformation.

"I attended a blockchain conference in Miami in 2017," recalled financial journalist Rebecca Winthrop. "The energy was indistinguishable from religious fervor. Speakers weren't just discussing an investment or technology—they were describing salvation from a corrupt system. The audience responded with the enthusiasm of converts."

When the inevitable crash came in 2018, with Bitcoin losing over 80% of its value, many observers predicted the end of the cryptocurrency experiment. But something curious happened: the core believers remained. They had seen this before—the boom-bust cycles that had taken Bitcoin from pennies to dollars, from dollars to hundreds, from hundreds to thousands. Each cycle brought new converts who stayed even after prices collapsed.

—

The COVID-19 pandemic and the subsequent flood of stimulus money created the conditions for Bitcoin's next metamorphosis. As governments printed trillions of dollars, the narrative of Bitcoin as "digital gold"—a hedge against inflation—gained traction among a new audience: institutional investors.

MicroStrategy CEO Michael Saylor converted his company's treasury reserves to Bitcoin, declaring it "a swarm of cyber hornets serving the goddess of wisdom, feeding on the fire of truth, exponentially growing ever smarter, faster, and stronger behind a wall of encrypted energy." The religious overtones were unmistakable.

Payment processors like PayPal and Square integrated cryptocurrency services. Wall Street firms that had once dismissed Bitcoin began offering it to clients. El Salvador adopted Bitcoin as legal tender. The outsider asset was being absorbed by the very system it was designed to challenge.

With this mainstreaming came tension within the community. Some celebrated the institutional adoption as validation of their early beliefs. Others worried that Bitcoin was being co-opted, stripped of its revolutionary potential and reduced to just another speculative asset class.

—-

What makes the Bitcoin phenomenon so revealing is not just the technology itself, but what it tells us about our relationship with financial systems. Like all bubbles, Bitcoin's price surges have been fueled by narrative. Unlike many bubbles, however, these narratives contained legitimate critiques of the existing order.

The central banks' response to the 2008 crisis had indeed created unprecedented distortions in financial markets. Wealth inequality had grown as asset prices soared while wages stagnated. Financial surveillance had expanded. Bitcoin's rise wasn't simply mass delusion—it was a response to real conditions.

"Every successful financial innovation addresses an unmet need," explained economist Martin Hargreaves. "Bitcoin emerged when trust in traditional financial institutions was at a historic low. Whether or not it succeeds in the long term, it revealed deep cracks in the legitimacy of our financial architecture."

The Bitcoin experiment also demonstrated how quickly new financial belief systems can form in the digital age. What took centuries for traditional financial institutions to build—trust, legitimacy, cultural acceptance—cryptocurrency achieved in just over a decade. The speed of this belief formation suggests both the fragility of our existing systems and the human capacity to reimagine them.

—-

As we watch Bitcoin and the broader cryptocurrency ecosystem continue to evolve, we're witnessing a fundamental tension play out: between the desire for financial sovereignty and the need for collective trust systems, between algorithmic certainty and human governance, between revolutionary ideals and institutional adoption.

The true significance of Bitcoin may not be whether it ultimately succeeds as a global currency or store of value. Rather, it may be that it demonstrated how quickly the social contracts underlying our financial systems can be questioned and reimagined when trust erodes.

In this way, Bitcoin serves as both warning and possibility—a reminder that money itself is ultimately a collective belief system, and that such beliefs can shift with remarkable speed when the conditions are right. Like the calm before other financial storms, the period of institutional skepticism toward Bitcoin has given way to cautious embrace, even as deeper questions about financial systems remain unanswered.

Whether Bitcoin represents the future of money or simply another chapter in the long history of financial manias, it has already succeeded in one crucial respect: forcing us to reconsider what money is, who should control it, and what happens when trust in its stewards begins to fail.

Chapter 17: Meme Stocks and Digital Crowds

In January 2021, on a cold Wednesday morning, the financial world witnessed something unprecedented. GameStop—a struggling brick-and-mortar video game retailer that most analysts had written off as another casualty of e-commerce—saw its stock price surge 135% in a single day. By week's end, it had climbed over 1,700%. Wall Street veterans watched in bewilderment as a company with declining revenues and no fundamental change in business prospects became the most actively traded stock in the United States.

This was not a traditional short squeeze engineered by sophisticated hedge funds. It was something altogether new: a digitally coordinated movement of retail investors, many using commission-free trading apps, who had organized themselves through social media—specifically, a forum on Reddit called WallStreetBets.

The air in the financial district felt different that week. Seasoned traders described it as disorienting, like the laws of financial gravity had been temporarily suspended. One hedge fund manager, speaking on condition of anonymity, told me: "It's like watching a game where suddenly everyone's playing by different rules, and those rules make no sense to us."

What made this moment significant wasn't just the dramatic price action. It was the emergence of a new kind of financial collective—one that operated through memes, inside jokes, and a shared narrative about taking revenge on Wall Street elites.

—-

To understand the meme stock phenomenon, we must first understand its context. The GameStop saga didn't emerge from nowhere. It was born in the particular soil of the post-2008 financial landscape, fertilized by more than a decade of quantitative easing, near-zero interest rates, and a growing generational divide in economic opportunity.

For many younger investors who came of age during the Great Recession, traditional financial advice seemed hollow. They had witnessed bailouts for banks while ordinary people lost homes. They had graduated into a job market where stable employment felt increasingly elusive. And they had watched as asset prices—particularly housing—climbed beyond their reach while their student debt accumulated.

"The system is rigged anyway," wrote one WallStreetBets user in a post that garnered thousands of upvotes. "So why not play the game differently?"

This sentiment—that the financial system operated by one set of rules for the powerful and another for everyone else—became the emotional foundation for what would follow. When these investors discovered that several hedge funds had taken massive short positions against GameStop, betting on its failure, they saw an opportunity not just for profit, but for a kind of financial justice.

—-

The mechanics of the GameStop event were relatively simple. Short sellers had borrowed and sold shares of GameStop, planning to buy them back later at a lower price. Their short interest had grown to more than 140% of available shares—meaning more shares had been sold short than actually existed. This created a potential for what traders call a "short squeeze," where rising prices force short sellers to buy shares to cover their positions, driving prices even higher.

What was new was the coordination mechanism. In previous eras, such collective action would have been nearly impossible to organize. But social media platforms, particularly Reddit, provided both the infrastructure for communication and the cultural context that made the movement coherent.

"What we're seeing is the democratization of financial information," explained Dr. Melissa Chen, a sociologist who studies online communities. "Financial knowledge that was once siloed in institutions is now being shared, debated, and acted upon by distributed networks of individuals."

The language of these online communities was distinctive—deliberately provocative, often crude, and peppered with terms like "tendies" (profits), "diamond hands" (holding through volatility), and "to the moon" (explosive price growth). This vernacular wasn't just colorful; it served to create in-group cohesion and distinguish community members from traditional financial professionals.

One 28-year-old participant I interviewed, a software engineer named Raj, explained: "The memes aren't just jokes. They're how we process information together. When someone posts a rocket emoji, it's shorthand for a complex set of beliefs about where the market is heading and why."

—-

What made these "meme stocks" different from previous speculative manias was their self-awareness. Unlike tulip buyers in 17th century Holland or day traders in 1999, many GameStop investors openly acknowledged the speculative nature of their actions. They weren't claiming that GameStop was fundamentally undervalued; they were explicitly betting on the power of collective action to move markets.

"We know this isn't about fundamentals," one popular post read. "It's about sending a message."

This message wasn't just directed at short-selling hedge funds. It was a broader statement about who gets to participate in financial markets and how. By deliberately adopting strategies that defied conventional wisdom, these investors were challenging the very notion of rational markets.

Traditional financial media struggled to make sense of it all. CNBC hosts appeared visibly frustrated trying to analyze stock movements that didn't respond to earnings reports or analyst ratings. One veteran market commentator lamented on air: "There's no way to model this. How do you factor 'Reddit enthusiasm' into a discounted cash flow analysis?"

The answer, of course, was that you couldn't. The meme stock phenomenon represented something markets had always contained but rarely acknowledged so openly: the power of narrative and collective belief.

—-

By February 2021, the GameStop frenzy had subsided somewhat. The stock, which had briefly touched $483, settled back below $100. Some investors had made life-changing money. Others had lost substantial sums. But the impact of what had occurred extended far beyond individual profit and loss statements.

The event triggered congressional hearings, regulatory discussions, and soul-searching throughout the financial industry. It raised fundamental questions about market structure, the role of social media in finance, and the changing relationship between retail and institutional investors.

Perhaps most significantly, it demonstrated how quickly new forms of financial coordination could emerge in the digital age. The same technologies that allow people to share cat videos or organize political movements could now be used to move billions of dollars through capital markets.

"What we witnessed wasn't just a short squeeze," noted Dr. Robert Shiller, the Nobel Prize-winning economist. "It was a demonstration of how financial markets have always been social constructs, driven by stories we tell ourselves and each other. The difference now is the speed and scale at which these stories can spread and evolve."

—-

The meme stock phenomenon didn't end with GameStop. In the months that followed, other companies with high short interest—AMC Entertainment, BlackBerry, Bed Bath & Beyond—experienced similar, if less dramatic, episodes. Each followed a similar pattern: online discussion building momentum, coordinated buying pressure, dramatic price spikes, and eventually, some degree of retracement.

What's particularly interesting about these events is how they blur the line between investment and social movement. For many participants, buying shares wasn't just about potential returns; it was about belonging to something larger than themselves. The act of purchasing stock became a form of digital solidarity, a way to vote with dollars against a system many felt had excluded them.

"I put in money I could afford to lose," explained Tasha, a 32-year-old nurse who bought GameStop shares at $220. "Even if it goes to zero, I felt like I was part of something important. How many investments can you say that about?"

This social dimension helps explain why many investors held onto their shares even as prices began to fall—a behavior that would be irrational in classical economic terms but made perfect sense within the cultural context of the movement. The community had developed its own metrics of success that weren't purely financial.

—-

As we reflect on the meme stock phenomenon from a historical perspective, certain parallels emerge with earlier financial manias. Like tulip buyers in 17th century Amsterdam or tech stock investors in

1999, meme stock traders were caught up in a powerful social current that temporarily suspended normal market dynamics.

Yet there are important differences. Unlike many historical bubbles, the meme stock movement was characterized by a high degree of self-awareness. Many participants openly acknowledged they were engaged in speculation rather than investment. There was also an explicit political dimension—a desire to challenge established power structures within financial markets.

Perhaps most significantly, the meme stock phenomenon revealed how technological change continues to reshape financial markets in ways that are difficult to predict. Just as the telegraph transformed 19th-century markets and electronic trading revolutionized 20th-century finance, social media platforms are now creating new possibilities for coordination among market participants.

This suggests that financial regulators and institutions must adapt to a world where market movements can originate not just from economic fundamentals or institutional decisions, but from distributed networks of individuals acting in concert through digital channels.

—-

As the dust settled on the initial GameStop saga, one hedge fund manager offered a perspective that seems particularly relevant: "What happened wasn't just about GameStop or even about Reddit. It was about the fact that markets are conversations. And the internet has changed who gets to participate in those conversations."

Indeed, the meme stock phenomenon may ultimately be remembered not for its impact on any particular company's stock price, but for how it democratized—for better or worse—the process of market narrative formation. Stories that once might have been crafted in boardrooms or on trading floors were now emerging from subreddits and Discord channels.

In this sense, meme stocks represent not just a financial curiosity but a shift in how collective beliefs about value are constructed and acted upon in the digital age. They remind us that markets have always been social institutions, reflecting not just economic realities but the stories we tell ourselves about those realities.

As we move forward, the boundary between social media and financial markets will likely continue to blur. New platforms, new forms of digital community, and new mechanisms for coordination will emerge. And with them will come new challenges for anyone seeking to understand—or predict—market behavior.

The calm surface of efficient markets has been disturbed, revealing the complex social currents that have always flowed beneath. In this new landscape, understanding human psychology, social dynamics, and digital culture may prove just as important as analyzing balance sheets or cash flows.

The meme stock phenomenon, like so many financial innovations before it, has changed the rules of the game. And as always, those who fail to adapt to these new rules do so at their own peril.

Chapter 18: WallStreetBets: Humor as Identity

In the winter of 2021, as pandemic lockdowns dragged on and stimulus checks arrived in American bank accounts, something remarkable happened in an obscure corner of the internet. A community that had been slowly growing for years suddenly found itself at the center of financial history. What began as a subreddit—an online forum dedicated to high-risk stock trading—transformed into a cultural phenomenon that would challenge Wall Street's fundamental assumptions about who controls market narratives.

WallStreetBets wasn't created to start a revolution. Founded in 2012 by Jaime Rogozinski, a then-30-year-old consultant, the forum began as a place where retail investors could discuss aggressive, often reckless trading strategies that would be dismissed on more conventional investment platforms. Its early members shared a gallows humor about their losses and occasional wins, posting screenshots of their trading accounts with a transparency that was both shocking and refreshing.

"I wanted a community where people could talk about high-risk trades in an unapologetic way," Rogozinski would later explain. "Everything else in finance is so careful, so politically correct."

What made WallStreetBets different from other investment communities wasn't just its tolerance for risk but its distinctive culture. While Wall Street prided itself on sophistication and exclusivity, WallStreetBets embraced a deliberately crass, self-deprecating humor. Members called themselves "degenerates" and "apes." They celebrated both spectacular gains ("tendies") and catastrophic losses ("loss porn") with equal enthusiasm. The community's unofficial mascot—a cartoon character with slicked-back hair and sunglasses known as the "Wall Street Bets guy"—embodied this devil-may-care ethos.

This wasn't just humor for humor's sake. It was identity formation.

"The language of WallStreetBets serves as both a barrier to entry and a badge of belonging," explained Dr. Gabriella Coleman, an anthropologist who studies online communities. "By developing their own vocabulary, they're defining who's in and who's out. It's tribal signaling."

The community's lexicon grew increasingly complex over time. A "YOLO" was a bet-it-all trade where someone invested their entire portfolio in a single high-risk position. "Diamond hands" meant holding onto a position despite volatility, while "paper hands" referred to selling too early. "Tendies" were profits, named after chicken tenders—the presumed meal of choice for successful traders. "FDs" were short-dated, out-of-the-money options contracts (the full term too profane for these pages).

This linguistic innovation wasn't merely colorful—it represented a fundamental reimagining of what investment discourse could sound like. Traditional financial media spoke in the language of careful analysis and measured expectations. WallStreetBets spoke in memes, jokes, and hyperbole. Where CNBC advised portfolio diversification, WallStreetBets celebrated concentration. Where financial advisors counseled long-term thinking, WallStreetBets reveled in the immediate dopamine hit of a risky bet paying off.

"We're not here to create generational wealth," wrote one popular poster in 2020. "We're here to feel something."

This sentiment captured a profound truth about the post-2008 financial landscape. For many younger investors who came of age during the Great Recession, the traditional financial system appeared fundamentally broken—promising rewards for prudence and patience that never seemed to materialize. If the system was rigged anyway, why not embrace the casino-like aspects of the market? Why not find community in the shared experience of financial roulette?

By early 2021, the subreddit had grown to over two million members. Then came GameStop.

The details of the GameStop short squeeze have been extensively documented elsewhere, but what's often overlooked is how humor functioned as the binding agent that held the movement together. As GameStop's stock price climbed from $20 to $40 to $100 and beyond, the forum exploded with memes celebrating the community's collective action against hedge funds that had heavily shorted the struggling video game retailer.

"What's happening isn't just a trade or an investment thesis," noted financial journalist Joe Weisenthal at the height of the frenzy. "It's a joke that got serious, then became a movement."

The jokes were everywhere. Members posted images of themselves with actual diamond hands. They shared videos of apes pounding their chests. They created elaborate movie parodies featuring hedge fund managers as villains. When Robinhood restricted trading in GameStop shares, the outrage was expressed not through formal complaints but through a tsunami of darkly comic memes about market manipulation.

This humor served multiple functions. First, it maintained morale during periods of extreme volatility. When the stock dropped 40% in a single day, the forum didn't panic—it posted memes about "buying the dip" and "holding the line." Second, it reinforced group solidarity against external criticism. When financial commentators dismissed the movement as irrational or dangerous, WallStreetBets responded with humor that mocked the critics' presumed expertise.

Most importantly, the humor acknowledged the absurdity of the situation while simultaneously treating it with deadly seriousness. Members could joke about "apes together strong"—a reference to the film "Planet of the Apes"—while genuinely believing in the collective power of retail investors to change market dynamics.

"What makes WallStreetBets powerful is that they're in on the joke, but the joke is also real," explained financial analyst Morgan Housel during the GameStop saga. "They're simultaneously self-aware about how ridiculous their approach is while being completely committed to it."

This paradoxical position—irony and sincerity occupying the same space—is characteristic of internet culture more broadly. But WallStreetBets applied it to finance in a way that traditional market participants struggled to comprehend. How could people make investment decisions based on memes? How could they risk their life savings while joking about it?

The answer lies in understanding that for many WallStreetBets participants, the community itself was as valuable as any potential financial gain. In a fractured, isolated world—particularly during pandemic lockdowns—the forum offered belonging, entertainment, and purpose. Members weren't just trading stocks; they were participating in a collective experience that gave meaning to otherwise abstract market movements.

"I made more friends during two weeks of the GameStop saga than in the previous year," one member told me. "We were all watching the same charts, feeling the same emotions, posting the same jokes. It felt like being part of something bigger than myself."

This social dimension helps explain why many members refused to sell even when GameStop reached astronomically high prices. Selling wasn't just a financial decision; it was a betrayal of the group. The humor reinforced this dynamic—those who sold early were mocked as having "paper hands," while those who held through massive drawdowns were celebrated for their "diamond hands."

The financial establishment never quite grasped this aspect of WallStreetBets. They analyzed the GameStop phenomenon through traditional metrics of valuation and rational actor theory. They missed that for many participants, the irrational exuberance was the point. The humor wasn't a side effect of the movement; it was its core.

As the GameStop saga eventually faded from headlines, WallStreetBets continued to evolve. Its membership swelled to over ten million, making it one of the largest financial communities in the world. Its influence spread to other stocks, cryptocurrencies, and even traditional media. Members appeared on financial news networks, launched their own trading platforms, and inspired academic studies on the democratization of finance.

But something was lost in this mainstreaming. As the community expanded, its distinctive humor began to dilute. New members arrived without understanding the cultural context that had made WallStreetBets unique. The inside jokes became more forced, the memes more derivative. Success had changed the very thing that made the forum special.

This is the paradox of all cultural movements that suddenly find themselves in the spotlight. The very attention that validates their significance also begins their transformation into something else. The humor that once defined a small, tight-knit community of risk-takers became commodified, packaged for broader consumption.

Yet the legacy of WallStreetBets extends beyond its specific impact on GameStop or any other stock. It demonstrated that in the internet age, market narratives can emerge from anywhere. The gatekeepers of financial information—analysts, financial media, institutional investors—no longer hold a monopoly on shaping market sentiment. A community united by shared jokes and a distinctive vocabulary can, under the right circumstances, move billions of dollars.

More profoundly, WallStreetBets revealed the extent to which all financial markets are social constructions—stories we collectively agree to believe. The humor of the forum worked precisely because it acknowledged this reality while traditional finance pretends otherwise. By treating the market as partly a game, partly a joke, and partly a battlefield, WallStreetBets members inadvertently exposed truths about market psychology that more "serious" investors often prefer to ignore.

In the quiet moments before the next financial storm, we would do well to remember this lesson. Behind the sophisticated models and confident projections of Wall Street analysts lies the same fundamental reality that WallStreetBets embraced: markets are human creations, driven by narratives, emotions, and social dynamics. Sometimes it takes a joke to reveal the most serious truths.

And in that recognition lies both warning and wisdom for whatever comes next.

Chapter 19: AI Fever

There is a particular quality to the light in Silicon Valley during the spring of 2023—a crystalline brightness that seems to illuminate not just the sprawling tech campuses and coffee shops, but the very faces of those who walk its streets. In Palo Alto cafés, in San Francisco co-working spaces, in venture capital offices along Sand Hill Road, conversations hum with an electric intensity. The words are different from those spoken during previous technology booms, but the cadence, the breathless enthusiasm, the wide-eyed certainty—these are familiar rhythms to anyone who has lived through cycles of technological euphoria.

"Have you tried the new GPT model?"

"We're pivoting the entire company to focus on AI."

"My friend's startup just raised fifty million on a deck that was basically 'ChatGPT for healthcare.'"

The arrival of sophisticated generative AI systems in late 2022 and early 2023 triggered something we have seen before: a moment when technology's potential seems to suddenly expand beyond all previous imagination. Like the arrival of the web browser in 1993, or the smartphone in 2007, these are inflection points when the future appears to arrive all at once, compressing years of anticipated development into months.

But there is something different about this particular fever—a strange intensity born from the intersection of several powerful forces: a tech industry desperate for a new narrative after the crypto winter and post-pandemic correction; abundant capital still searching for returns in a high-interest environment; and genuinely remarkable technology that seemed to leap from research papers to consumer products with unprecedented speed.

—-

To understand AI fever, we must first understand what preceded it. The 2010s had been dominated by the rise of social media, mobile applications, and cloud computing—technologies that transformed how we communicate, shop, and work. By the late 2010s, these technologies had matured, and the industry was searching for its next frontier.

Cryptocurrency and Web3 briefly captured this energy, promising a decentralized digital future. But by 2022, that narrative had collapsed under the weight of falling prices, fraud scandals, and a growing sense that the technology's practical applications remained elusive. Silicon Valley found itself in an unusual position: uncertain about its next chapter.

Then came the public release of ChatGPT in November 2022.

"It was like watching the first iPhone demo all over again," recalled one veteran venture capitalist who had funded companies through multiple tech cycles. "That moment when you realize everything is about to change, and you're both thrilled and terrified of being left behind."

Within weeks, Microsoft had invested billions in OpenAI. Google declared a "code red" and rushed to release its own AI systems. Venture capital, which had been retreating from the market, suddenly flowed back in torrents. Startups with "AI" in their pitch decks saw their valuations double, then triple. Engineers with machine learning expertise became the most sought-after talent in an industry that had been conducting layoffs just months earlier.

By spring 2023, Nvidia—the company making the specialized chips required for AI development—had become the world's most valuable company, surging past the trillion-dollar mark. Its stock price moved with the fevered rhythm that market historians recognize from previous manias: near-vertical ascents that defy traditional valuation metrics.

"The numbers don't matter anymore," a hedge fund manager told me over coffee in Manhattan. "This is about owning a piece of the future. You can't price that with a discounted cash flow model."

—-

The most striking aspect of AI fever isn't just the money—though the sums are staggering—but the psychological transformation it represents. Suddenly, executives who had never shown interest in artificial intelligence were restructuring entire corporations around it. Companies added "AI" to their names and saw their stock prices jump, echoing the dot-com era when similar rebranding around the internet produced the same effect.

What makes this particular fever so potent is that, unlike some previous technological manias, the underlying technology is genuinely transformative. The large language models and image generation systems released during this period can perform tasks that seemed impossible just years earlier. They write code, create images, summarize documents, and engage in conversations with a fluency that astonishes even AI researchers.

But as with all fevers, AI's rise generated its own peculiar distortions of thought and perception.

In Midtown Manhattan, I met with the CEO of a 30-year-old software company who had just announced an "AI transformation" that sent his company's stock up 40% in a single day.

"Between us," he said, lowering his voice despite the private setting, "we're doing exactly what we were doing six months ago, just repackaging it. But if I don't use the AI narrative, I'm dead in this market."

At a conference in Boston, I watched as a panel of healthcare executives competed to outdo each other with AI superlatives:

"AI will completely transform patient care within five years."

"We're looking at the end of diagnostic errors as we know them."

"This is as significant as the discovery of antibiotics."

These statements weren't necessarily false—AI may indeed transform healthcare—but the certainty with which they were delivered, the absence of nuance or caution, carried the unmistakable markers of fever thinking.

—-

Like all financial and technological fevers, the AI boom carries within it both genuine innovation and the seeds of excess. The pattern is as old as markets themselves: a transformative technology emerges, capital rushes in, valuations detach from fundamentals, a correction eventually follows. What makes each cycle unique isn't the pattern itself, but the particular character of the technology and the social context in which it emerges.

What distinguishes AI fever is the existential dimension it carries. Unlike previous technological revolutions, artificial intelligence raises profound questions about the nature of human work, creativity, and even consciousness. The fever isn't just about money or convenience—it's about our place in a world where machines can increasingly do what we thought only humans could do.

In San Francisco, I spoke with a group of programmers at a bar near the Embarcadero. They had been discussing the implications of AI for their careers.

"I've spent fifteen years mastering my craft," said one, a software engineer at a major tech company. "Now I watch ChatGPT write code that would have taken me hours to produce. What happens when it gets ten times better? A hundred times better?"

His colleague, nursing a beer, nodded slowly. "But we're also using it to become super-developers. I'm twice as productive with these tools. It's augmentation, not replacement."

"For now," the first engineer replied.

Their conversation captures the peculiar mixture of excitement and anxiety that permeates AI fever—the sense that we are witnessing something that will transform not just industries but the very nature of human work and creativity.

—-

History suggests that all fevers eventually break. The question isn't whether AI fever will moderate, but how and when—and what will remain after the temperature returns to normal.

Will AI follow the path of the internet—a technology that, despite the dot-com bubble and crash, genuinely transformed our world in ways that exceeded even the most optimistic early predictions? Or will it follow the path of technologies like virtual reality, which has seen multiple cycles of hype and disappointment without achieving its promised revolution?

The most likely outcome lies somewhere between these extremes. Artificial intelligence will indeed transform many industries and aspects of daily life, but perhaps not as completely or as quickly as the fever dream suggests. Some AI startups will justify their astronomical valuations; many others will not. Some jobs will be transformed or eliminated; others will prove more resistant to automation than expected.

What remains certain is that we are witnessing one of history's recurring moments when technology, capital, and human psychology converge to create a period of extraordinary possibility and risk. In these moments, the line between visionary insight and delusion becomes vanishingly thin. The same pattern of thinking that leads to breakthrough innovation also produces spectacular miscalculations.

As one venture capitalist told me, "In every boom, the right people are making the right bets for the wrong reasons, and the wrong people are making the wrong bets for the right reasons. The trick is figuring out which is which before everyone else does."

For now, AI fever continues to burn bright, transforming companies, careers, and capital allocations at a pace that leaves many breathless. Like all fevers, it reveals as much about our hopes, fears, and collective psychology as it does about the technology itself. And like all fevers that have come before, it offers both opportunity and warning to those who can maintain their perspective while all around them lose theirs.

In the quiet moments between the breathless headlines and funding announcements, a more nuanced reality is taking shape—one where artificial intelligence neither saves humanity nor replaces it, but instead becomes integrated into our world in ways both more profound and more mundane than the fever dreams suggest. This is the pattern of technological revolution: the reality always differs from both the hype and the fear, yet ultimately transforms us nonetheless.

Chapter 20: Every Bubble Needs a Story

In the quiet reading room of the New York Public Library, there is a collection of newspapers from October 1929. Yellowed with age, their headlines trumpet the soundness of the market just days before its historic collapse. These pages are not merely historical curiosities—they are artifacts of narrative, fragments of a story that millions of Americans had collectively agreed to believe.

Every financial bubble throughout history has been, at its core, a story that captured the imagination. Not merely a deception or a lie, but a narrative powerful enough to suspend disbelief, to transform how we see value, and to justify behavior that would, in ordinary times, seem plainly irrational.

Consider the strange life cycle of these stories. They begin modestly, anchored in some genuine innovation or change. The tulip, arriving in the Netherlands from the Ottoman Empire, was indeed a botanical marvel. The internet of the 1990s truly did represent a revolution in human communication. Housing has always been a fundamental human need. Bitcoin's blockchain technology genuinely offered a novel approach to trust in digital transactions. Each artificial intelligence breakthrough does expand the boundaries of what machines can accomplish.

The initial story is not false. It is simply incomplete.

As these narratives gain momentum, they undergo a subtle transformation. The story shifts from the specific to the universal, from the concrete to the abstract. It is no longer about a particular technology or asset, but about a new paradigm, a fundamental shift in how the world works.

"This time is different," we tell ourselves, five words that Sir John Templeton called the most expensive in the English language.

During the South Sea Bubble of 1720, investors poured money into a company whose operations in South America remained deliberately vague. The company's promoters understood that specificity was the enemy of speculation. The less defined the story, the more room for the investor's imagination to fill in the details with dreams of untold riches.

In the dot-com era, the narrative evolved from "the internet will change communication" (true) to "any company with a '.com' in its name will inevitably succeed" (false). The story's power grew even as its connection to reality weakened. Pets.com, with its sock puppet mascot and business model that lost money on every sale, raised $82.5 million in its IPO before collapsing nine months later.

The housing bubble transformed from "real estate is a sound long-term investment" to "housing prices can only go up." The story became self-reinforcing, as rising prices seemed to validate the narrative, drawing in more believers, pushing prices higher still, in a feedback loop that seemed to defy gravity.

What makes these narratives so powerful is not merely greed, though that certainly plays a role. It is that they offer a coherent framework for understanding a changing world. They provide certainty in uncertain times. They transform complexity into simplicity. Most importantly, they offer membership in a community of believers.

During the GameStop phenomenon of 2021, many participants openly acknowledged they were participating in something irrational. "I'm not selling even if it goes to zero," they proclaimed on Reddit forums. The point wasn't the investment thesis—it was belonging to a movement, being part of a collective story about outsiders challenging the system.

These narratives spread through social contagion. In 17th century Amsterdam, tulip mania spread through taverns and coffee houses. The 1920s stock boom traveled through ticker tape and newspaper columns. The dot-com bubble expanded through CNBC and early internet message boards. Today's investment narratives propagate at the speed of social media, mutating and amplifying as they spread.

What makes a bubble narrative particularly dangerous is that it contains enough truth to be plausible. The internet did change everything. Housing is essential. Blockchain is innovative. Artificial intelligence is transformative. The kernel of truth at the center makes the speculative excess around it easier to accept.

We can see this pattern clearly in the AI boom of 2022-2023. The technology itself represents a genuine breakthrough. ChatGPT and similar systems demonstrated capabilities that surprised even experts in the field. But the narrative quickly expanded beyond the technology itself to encompass a complete reimagining of the economy, society, and even what it means to be human.

Companies with no meaningful AI capabilities added the term to their names and saw their stock prices soar. Venture capitalists who had just recovered from crypto losses rushed to fund anything with "artificial intelligence" in the pitch deck. The story became not just about a specific technology but about an inevitable future—a narrative of destiny rather than possibility.

This is the paradox of bubble narratives: they begin with innovation but end with orthodoxy. What starts as a novel idea becomes an unquestionable truth. The story calcifies from "this could change things" to "this will change everything" to "this has already changed everything, and you're either with us or against us."

The most telling sign of a bubble narrative reaching its final stage is when skepticism is no longer treated as prudence but as heresy. When those who question the story are not engaged with but excluded, not debated but dismissed. The dot-com skeptics were "dinosaurs who don't get it." Housing bubble doubters "didn't understand the new financial instruments." Cryptocurrency critics were "nocoiners" who would regret their hesitation. AI skeptics are characterized as fearful Luddites standing in the way of progress.

In each case, the narrative becomes not just an investment thesis but an identity. To question the story is to question the community itself.

This is not to say that every powerful market narrative ends in disaster. Some transformative technologies do indeed change the world and create enormous value. The internet, despite the dot-com crash, did revolutionize business and society. The question is not whether the core innovation is real, but whether the financial expectations surrounding it have detached from reasonable projections of future value.

The most dangerous moment comes when the narrative no longer needs facts to sustain it—when it becomes self-referential, drawing its strength not from external validation but from the collective belief of its adherents. When the story itself becomes the evidence.

In the quiet before financial storms, these narratives reach their peak potency. They become totalizing, explaining everything, answering all doubts. They create their own gravity, pulling in not just individual investors but institutions, policymakers, and cultural figures.

And then, often with surprising swiftness, they collapse. Not because the innovation at their core was worthless, but because no innovation could possibly live up to the expectations that the narrative had created. The story falls apart not because it was entirely false, but because it was incomplete—it left out the constraints, the complications, the contradictions that exist in any human endeavor.

After the collapse, we look back and wonder how we could have believed such things. We distance ourselves from our former certainty. We claim we always had doubts. We rewrite our own histories.

Until the next story comes along, offering a new lens through which to see the world, a new community to join, a new certainty in uncertain times. And the cycle begins again, not as repetition, but as rhyme—familiar enough to be recognized by those who remember, novel enough to convince those who don't that this time, truly, is different.

The power of these narratives reveals something profound about markets and human nature. Markets are not merely mechanisms for price discovery—they are arenas of storytelling, places where we collectively author the narratives that shape our economic lives. And in those stories, we reveal not just our hopes for wealth, but our deeper longings for meaning, community, and certainty in an uncertain world.

Chapter 21: Cheap Money and the Cost We Don't See

Money has always been a strange abstraction—a promise written on paper, a number in a ledger, a shared illusion we collectively agree to believe. But something fundamental changed in our relationship with money after the 2008 financial crisis. Money became not just abstract but abundant, at least in certain circles. The cost of borrowing it fell to near zero, and in some cases, below zero. This was the era of what economists call "cheap money," and like most things that become suddenly inexpensive, we began to use it differently.

In the quiet halls of central banks around the world, a grand experiment was underway. The Federal Reserve, the European Central Bank, the Bank of Japan, and others had opened the floodgates of liquidity to prevent economic collapse. Interest rates were slashed to historic lows. Quantitative easing—that clinical term for creating money to buy financial assets—expanded central bank balance sheets to sizes previously unimaginable.

The intention was noble: prevent a second Great Depression. And by that measure, it worked. The financial system did not collapse. Unemployment, while devastating, did not reach the apocalyptic levels of the 1930s. The emergency measures succeeded in their immediate goal.

But cheap money, like all powerful medicines, came with side effects—some obvious, others subtle, and many that we're still trying to understand.

—-

On a spring morning in 2012, David Mendelson, a thirty-four-year-old software engineer in San Francisco, received an email from his bank. The mortgage rate he had locked in six months earlier at what seemed an impossibly low 4.2% could now be refinanced at 3.1%. With a few clicks and some paperwork, his monthly payment would drop by nearly $400.

"It felt like finding money on the sidewalk," David told me years later. "I kept waiting for someone to tell me there was a catch."

There wasn't a catch—not for David, at least. His story repeated millions of times across America as homeowners with good credit and stable jobs found themselves awash in financial opportunity. The monthly savings were real. The additional purchasing power was real. The wealth effect as home values rose again was real.

Across town, Jessica Ramirez, a dental assistant who rented a one-bedroom apartment, experienced a different reality. Her student loan payments remained fixed. Her rent increased by 7% that year, and would continue to rise each year thereafter. The economy was supposedly recovering, but her financial breathing room narrowed.

"Everyone kept talking about how cheap money was," she recalled. "But not for me. Not for people like me."

This divergence—between those with access to cheap money and those without—represents the first hidden cost of the era: the widening of existing inequalities.

—-

The mathematics of near-zero interest rates transformed not just personal finance but the very logic of capitalism. When borrowing costs almost nothing, the time horizon for investment returns stretches toward infinity. Projects that might have seemed foolish in a normal interest rate environment suddenly appeared rational.

Consider what happened in corporate America. Companies could borrow billions at historically low rates. The prudent approach might have been to invest this windfall in research, worker training, or productivity-enhancing equipment. Some did. But many found a more immediately rewarding strategy: borrowing money to buy back their own stock.

Between 2009 and 2019, American corporations spent over $5 trillion repurchasing their own shares—an amount that exceeded all other forms of capital expenditure combined. This financial engineering boosted stock prices and executive compensation packages tied to share performance. It did not, however, necessarily improve the underlying productive capacity of these firms.

"We created a system where the rational decision for a CEO was often financial engineering rather than actual engineering," explained Robert Shiller, the Nobel Prize-winning economist, when I interviewed him. "The incentives became misaligned with long-term economic health."

This misalignment represents the second hidden cost: the diversion of capital from productive investment to financial optimization.

—-

Perhaps the most profound cost of cheap money lies in how it altered our perception of risk. When central banks repeatedly intervened to prevent market downturns—the so-called "Fed put"—investors learned to expect rescue. Risk became something to embrace rather than manage.

In the mountain town of Jackson Hole, Wyoming, where central bankers gather annually to discuss monetary policy, I once asked a Federal Reserve official about this concern. Speaking on condition of anonymity, he acknowledged the dilemma.

"We're aware of the moral hazard," he said, using the economist's term for when protection from risk encourages riskier behavior. "But when you're facing potential systemic collapse, you don't have the luxury of worrying about the long-term behavioral implications. You put out the fire first."

The fire was extinguished, but something changed in our collective psychology. Financial markets came to operate with an implicit guarantee—a belief that downside risk was limited by the willingness of central banks to intervene. This led to what economists call "risk compression," where assets that should carry different risk profiles begin to trade as if they were equally safe.

High-yield bonds, emerging market debt, technology stocks with no earnings—all saw their risk premiums shrink. The market no longer efficiently distinguished between the sturdy oak and the fragile sapling. Everything was valued as if winter would never come.

—-

The term "zombie company" entered the financial lexicon during this period—firms that generate just enough cash flow to service their debt but not enough to invest or grow, essentially walking dead, kept alive only by cheap credit. By some estimates, up to 15% of publicly traded companies in developed economies fell into this category by 2020.

In normal times, these companies would have failed, their resources reallocated to more productive enterprises. Creative destruction—the process by which the new replaces the old—is essential to economic vitality. But cheap money interrupted this cycle, preserving the status quo and preventing the renewal that comes through failure.

"We've suspended the natural selection of capitalism," explained Karen Harris, managing director of Bain & Company's Macro Trends Group. "That feels compassionate in the short run—who wants to see businesses fail and people lose jobs? But it may be crueler in the long run if it means we're preserving inefficiency and blocking innovation."

This preservation of the unproductive represents the third hidden cost: the zombification of parts of the economy.

—-

When something becomes abundant, we value it differently. Think of water in a desert versus water by a lake. Scarcity shapes our perception of worth. As money became abundant for certain classes of borrowers, our relationship with it changed. Patient capital—money willing to wait for returns—became impatient. Long-term thinking shortened.

In venture capital, where I spent time observing the transformation, the conversation shifted from "Is this a sustainable business?" to "How quickly can we scale and exit?" Companies that might have grown organically over decades were pushed to expand at breakneck speed, often at the expense of building durable foundations.

"We're not building cathedrals anymore," a veteran venture capitalist told me over coffee in Palo Alto. "We're building movie sets—things that look impressive from the front but have nothing behind them. The goal isn't to create something that lasts a hundred years. It's to create something that looks good enough to sell next year."

This shift in time horizons represents the fourth hidden cost: the devaluation of durability and patience.

—-

The most insidious cost of cheap money may be what it did to our perception of value itself. When asset prices rise consistently year after year—not because of improved productivity or innovation, but because of monetary conditions—we begin to lose our bearings about what things are worth.

Is a house in San Francisco really "worth" a million dollars, or is that just the price determined by cheap mortgages and limited supply? Is a digital token representing a cartoon ape really "worth" hundreds of thousands of dollars, or is that a function of speculative excess fueled by abundant liquidity?

When money loses its scarcity value, it becomes a less reliable measuring stick. This distortion affects not just financial decisions but life decisions. Young people choose careers based on which will help them afford housing in markets inflated by cheap money. Retirees find their carefully planned savings generating insufficient income, pushing them toward riskier investments.

"We've lost our ability to value things intrinsically," observed William White, former chief economist at the Bank for International Settlements. "When everything is measured against a ruler made of rubber, you get very strange measurements."

—-

As this chapter is being written, the era of cheap money appears to be ending. Central banks, confronted with inflation they long insisted was "transitory," have raised interest rates significantly. The medicine that treated the last crisis has created side effects that require their own treatment.

But the legacy of cheap money will remain with us for years to come. The debts accumulated during this period must still be serviced. The behavioral patterns established over more than a decade will not disappear overnight. The inequalities that widened may narrow somewhat but will not automatically close.

Perhaps most importantly, we have yet to fully reckon with how this unprecedented monetary experiment changed our relationship with money itself—how it altered our perception of risk, our time horizons, our sense of what constitutes value.

The visible benefits of cheap money were immediate and tangible: economic collapse was averted, jobs were preserved, wealth was created. The costs were delayed, diffuse, and often invisible—until suddenly, they weren't.

As we transition to whatever monetary regime comes next, we would do well to remember that money is never truly "cheap." Someone, somewhere, always pays the price. The question is whether we see the cost in time to learn from it.

Chapter 22: The Joy of Collective Belief

There is something profoundly human about believing together.

When we stand in a stadium, surrounded by thousands chanting the same anthem, we feel it. When we join a religious congregation in prayer, we know it. And when we participate in a rising market that seems destined only to climb higher, we experience a particular form of this collective euphoria—one that binds strangers together in a shared vision of the future.

Financial bubbles are not merely economic phenomena. They are social experiences—moments when individual decisions merge into something greater, when personal hopes align with collective dreams. The emotional power of these moments should not be underestimated or dismissed as mere irrationality. There is a joy in collective belief that transcends the cold mathematics of return on investment.

Consider the crypto conferences of 2017, when Bitcoin approached $20,000 for the first time. Attendees described a feeling of participating in something revolutionary—not just a new asset class, but a reimagining of money itself. The energy in convention centers from Miami to Tokyo crackled with possibility. Strangers became instant confidants, sharing stories of financial liberation and technological revolution. The standard greeting—"When did you get in?"—was an invitation to share personal testimony, to locate oneself within a collective narrative.

"I felt like I was part of history," one early Bitcoin investor told me. "Not just making money, though that was happening too, but witnessing the birth of something that would change everything. The people around me felt it too. We weren't just investors—we were believers."

This sense of shared purpose is not unique to cryptocurrency. During the housing boom of the early 2000s, real estate seminars transformed ordinary people into enthusiastic investors. The language shifted subtly from homes as places to live to houses as vehicles for wealth creation. Attendees nodded in recognition as speakers validated what everyone seemed to already know: real estate only goes up. The fellowship of the converted provided not just investment strategies but belonging—a community united by insider knowledge.

The dot-com era offered similar communion. The New Economy was not merely a market thesis but an identity. Those who understood the transformative power of the internet were not just making financial decisions; they were aligning themselves with the future. The shared vocabulary—"eyeballs," "stickiness," "first-mover advantage"—served as signals of belonging. To question the valuation of a company with no profits was to reveal oneself as someone who "didn't get it," who stood outside the circle of understanding.

This collective experience creates a powerful feedback loop. The more people who believe, the more valid the belief appears. Markets, after all, move on consensus. If enough people believe something is valuable, it becomes valuable—at least for a time. This self-reinforcing dynamic helps explain why bubbles can expand far beyond what fundamental analysis would suggest is reasonable.

But the joy of collective belief goes deeper than financial validation. It offers meaning in an increasingly fragmented world. In an age of dissolving institutions and weakening traditional bonds, market movements provide a rare opportunity for shared experience across geographic, political, and cultural divides. The WallStreetBets community demonstrated this power vividly during the GameStop phenomenon—strangers united not just by potential profit but by a shared identity, complete with its own language, symbols, and heroes.

"It wasn't about the money," one Reddit user explained after the GameStop rally. "I mean, it was partly about the money. But it was more about being part of something bigger than myself. For once, I felt connected to thousands of others. We were in it together."

This sense of togetherness can be particularly potent during times of social isolation or institutional distrust. The cryptocurrency surge during the COVID-19 pandemic wasn't coincidental—it offered community when physical gathering was impossible and a narrative of financial self-determination when many felt powerless.

There is also a distinct pleasure in the acceleration of time that accompanies market manias. Normal life unfolds gradually, with achievements measured in years and decades. But during speculative booms, fortunes can change overnight. Friends become millionaires in weeks. Companies reach valuations in months that once took decades to achieve. This compression of time creates a heightened state of awareness—a collective present tense where possibility seems unlimited.

"Everything was happening so fast," recalled a tech worker who lived through the late 1990s boom in San Francisco. "You'd go to sleep and wake up to a different world. It was exhausting but exhilarating. We all felt it—this sense that we were living in fast-forward, that a decade was happening in a year."

The euphoria of these moments is real, and the connections formed are genuine. But there is a shadow side to collective belief. The same social dynamics that create belonging also enforce conformity. As bubbles inflate, skepticism becomes increasingly unwelcome. Those who question the prevailing narrative find themselves excluded, their concerns dismissed as fear or failure of imagination.

During the housing boom, mortgage brokers who expressed concern about lending standards were sidelined. In crypto circles, the term "nocoiners" emerged to describe those who hadn't bought in—not just financially but ideologically. The dot-com era had its "old economy" thinkers who "just didn't understand." This marginalization of dissent isn't merely incidental; it's essential to maintaining the collective belief that drives prices higher.

The joy of believing together also carries within it the seeds of collective disappointment. When bubbles eventually burst—as they invariably do—the shared narrative collapses. The community that formed around rising prices dissolves. The language that once signaled belonging becomes a reminder of collective miscalculation.

Yet even in the aftermath, participants often recall the experience with a complex nostalgia. They may regret financial losses but remember fondly the sense of possibility, the accelerated time, the feeling of being part of something larger than themselves. This emotional residue explains why, despite repeated cycles of boom and bust, new generations eagerly embrace the next compelling narrative.

Perhaps we should view these episodes not merely as market failures but as expressions of a deeply human need—the desire to believe together, to participate in a story larger than our individual lives. Financial markets, with their blend of mathematical precision and narrative power, offer a unique canvas for collective imagination.

Understanding this social dimension of markets doesn't prevent bubbles, but it helps explain their persistent recurrence. As we navigate the current landscape of AI enthusiasm, meme stocks, or whatever narrative captures collective imagination next, we might recognize that what drives these movements isn't just greed or irrationality. It's also the profound joy of believing together—a joy that connects us to one another and to a future we can imagine collectively.

The markets, in their strange way, offer us what we've always sought: not just wealth, but belonging. Not just returns, but meaning. Not just transactions, but transformation. The joy of collective belief may lead to financial excess, but it speaks to something essential in our nature—our need to share stories about what might be possible.

Chapter 23: The Fear of Missing Out

There is a particular anxiety that blooms during the final stages of a market's ascent—a sensation both electric and uncomfortable. It has always existed, but only recently acquired its modern name: FOMO, the fear of missing out. This emotion, more than greed or optimism, drives the last and most dramatic phase of market euphorias.

In the winter of 1636, Dutch merchants who had previously dismissed tulip speculation as foolishness found themselves unable to bear the stories of neighbors who had purchased entire houses with profits from a single bulb. In 1929, taxi drivers and housekeepers opened brokerage accounts after hearing how acquaintances had doubled their money in weeks. In 1999, conservative investors who had avoided technology stocks all decade finally capitulated as they watched college dropouts become paper millionaires overnight.

The psychology is remarkably consistent across centuries. FOMO begins not with desire for wealth, but with the human need to belong. To stand apart from a collective excitement is to experience a particular kind of social isolation—the feeling of watching a celebration through a window, uninvited and unacknowledged.

"I knew it was probably too late," recalled Marcus Ellington, a 62-year-old retired accountant who bought his first Bitcoin in December 2017, near its then-peak of nearly $20,000. "But everyone at my grandson's birthday party was talking about their crypto wallets. My brother-in-law, who never had two nickels to rub together, was showing everyone screenshots of his Coinbase account. I felt like the only person who wasn't part of this new world."

The fear of missing out operates most powerfully when it creates the sense that a fundamental shift is occurring—that the world is being divided into those who understand the new paradigm and those who don't. During the GameStop phenomenon, this division was explicit and celebrated. The members of WallStreetBets proudly distinguished themselves from the "boomers" who couldn't grasp their movement. The language, the memes, the strategy—all created boundaries between insiders and outsiders.

What makes FOMO particularly dangerous is how it distorts rational decision-making. Studies in behavioral economics have demonstrated that humans feel the pain of losses approximately twice as intensely as the pleasure of equivalent gains. But FOMO inverts this equation by reframing inaction itself as a form of loss—the loss of potential gains, the loss of status, the loss of belonging to the vanguard.

"The mathematics of FOMO are peculiar," explains Dr. Elaine Chen, behavioral economist at Princeton University. "When you're watching others gain 20% a month while you earn nothing, that zero begins to feel like negative 20%. Your unchanged position feels like active decline."

This psychological distortion explains why market bubbles accelerate in their final stages. The initial rise might be driven by legitimate innovation or changing fundamentals, but the steepest ascents—the nearly vertical lines on the charts—are fueled by the rush of latecomers desperate not to be left behind.

During the housing boom of 2004-2006, this dynamic played out in living rooms across America. Young couples who had initially resisted buying at inflated prices found themselves contemplating a disturbing possibility: if they didn't act soon, they might never own a home. The fear wasn't just about missing investment returns—it was existential, about being permanently excluded from the American dream.

"We looked at houses for three years," remembered Sarah Denton of Phoenix, Arizona. "Each time we hesitated, the prices jumped another fifty thousand dollars. Eventually, we convinced ourselves that waiting was the risky choice. Everyone said housing only goes up. My parents, our friends, even our financial advisor said we needed to get on the property ladder before it was too late."

The Dentons purchased their home in February 2007, just months before the market began its historic collapse.

What makes FOMO particularly powerful is how it combines with another psychological tendency: the substitution of social proof for personal analysis. When uncertain about complex matters, humans naturally look to others for guidance. This adaptive shortcut serves us well in many contexts but becomes dangerous in markets where collective behavior can detach from fundamental reality.

During the AI investment surge of 2023, countless retail investors admitted they didn't fully understand the technology or business models they were betting on. Their investment thesis was essentially: "Smarter people than me are excited about this." When enough participants rely on this logic, markets can sustain themselves on circular reasoning—people are buying because others are buying.

The digital acceleration of FOMO represents perhaps the most significant change in market psychology of the past decade. Previous manias spread through personal conversations, newspaper reports, and later, television. Today's spread through social media, with algorithms specifically designed to amplify emotional content and create engagement through envy and aspiration.

"I remember exactly when I broke down and bought Dogecoin," said Tyler Weston, a 29-year-old graphic designer. "I was scrolling through Instagram at 2 AM, seeing story after story of people my age celebrating their crypto gains. One guy I barely knew from college posted about paying off his student loans with Doge profits. The next morning, I put in three thousand dollars—money I'd been saving for a down payment. Two weeks later, it was worth less than half that."

What Tyler experienced wasn't just envy—it was a manufactured emotion, amplified by platforms designed to maximize engagement through comparison. The constant visibility of others' success creates an ambient pressure that previous generations of investors never faced.

The fear of missing out has always existed, but never before has it been so deliberately cultivated, so instantly transmitted, so globally synchronized. This may explain why modern market cycles appear to be compressing—why bubbles form and burst with increasing frequency.

Yet for all its power, FOMO contains the seeds of its own resolution. The more people who act based on the fear of missing out, the fewer remain on the sidelines. When the last skeptic capitulates, when the final holdout invests, the market runs out of new participants. The music doesn't stop because someone decides to turn it off—it stops because the room is already full, with everyone already dancing.

In this way, FOMO creates the very conditions that ensure its participants will, eventually, miss out after all.

Chapter 24: Confidence as a Currency

In the autumn of 1929, just days before the great crash, Yale economist Irving Fisher declared that stock prices had reached "what looks like a permanently high plateau." His words, spoken with the full weight of academic authority, have echoed through history not as wisdom but as a warning about the fragility of certainty. Fisher was not merely wrong—he was wrong at precisely the moment when his confidence carried the most consequence.

Confidence is not merely an emotion that accompanies economic activity. It is, in many ways, the primary currency of markets themselves—a medium of exchange that can appreciate and depreciate, that can be hoarded or spent lavishly, and that can evaporate with startling speed.

Unlike physical currency, which maintains its material form even as its value fluctuates, confidence leaves no trace when it vanishes. One day it fills the air like oxygen, taken for granted and seemingly permanent. The next day it is simply gone, leaving only questions about how something so substantial could disappear so completely.

Consider how markets operate in their most fundamental form. When we strip away the complexity of derivatives, algorithms, and financial engineering, markets remain what they have always been: conversations about the future conducted through the language of price. And these conversations require confidence to function at all.

The word "credit" itself comes from the Latin *credere*—to believe or trust. Every loan, every investment, every transaction beyond simple barter rests on this foundation. We accept currency because we trust in its future acceptance by others. We invest because we believe in future returns. We extend credit because we expect future repayment. Without these beliefs—without confidence—the machinery of commerce would grind to a halt.

This is why central banks guard their credibility with such vigilance. When Federal Reserve Chairman Paul Volcker raised interest rates to unprecedented levels in the early 1980s to combat inflation, he was not simply adjusting monetary policy. He was rebuilding the currency of confidence that had been depleted during the inflationary spiral of the 1970s. The economic pain was severe, but the restoration of confidence proved essential for sustainable growth.

What makes confidence so powerful—and so dangerous—is its self-reinforcing nature. Confidence creates the conditions for its own validation, just as its absence confirms its own disappearance. This circular quality gives markets their momentum in both directions.

During the housing boom of the mid-2000s, confidence in ever-rising home prices made those very increases possible. Banks lent freely against appreciating collateral. Homeowners borrowed against growing equity. Developers built with abandon. Each participant's confidence validated and amplified the confidence of others, creating a feedback loop that seemed to defy economic gravity.

Until it didn't.

When confidence begins to waver, its decline follows the same self-reinforcing pattern, but in reverse. The first signs are subtle—a hesitation in lending, a slight uptick in inventory, a small increase in time-on-market. These signals, barely perceptible at first, begin to compound. Caution breeds more caution. Hesitation spreads like contagion.

What makes this process particularly treacherous is that confidence often appears strongest precisely when it is most vulnerable. The peak of market euphoria—when confidence is most visibly abundant—is exactly when it has been stretched to its thinnest, most fragile state.

This paradox explains why market tops rarely announce themselves clearly. At these moments, confidence is simultaneously ubiquitous and precarious—like ice that appears most solid just before the spring thaw reveals its fatal thinning.

The digital age has accelerated and amplified these dynamics. Information now travels at the speed of light rather than the speed of gossip. Sentiment can shift globally in hours rather than weeks. The WallStreetBets phenomenon demonstrated how quickly confidence can coalesce around a narrative and mobilize capital. The cryptocurrency markets have shown how rapidly valuation paradigms can form, collapse, and reform.

Yet despite these technological accelerations, the fundamental nature of confidence remains unchanged. It still requires maintenance. It still demands periodic validation. And it still vanishes faster than it forms.

This asymmetry—the slow building and rapid collapse of confidence—creates the characteristic pattern of market cycles. Bull markets climb a wall of worry, gradually converting skeptics into believers over months or years. Bear markets descend a slope of hope, rapidly transforming optimists into pessimists over days or weeks.

Understanding confidence as currency helps explain why economic forecasting so often fails at crucial junctures. Traditional economic models struggle to quantify the ebbs and flows of collective belief. They can measure the tangible results of confidence—spending patterns, investment flows, credit creation—but not confidence itself.

This limitation becomes most problematic during major transitions, when the relationship between economic fundamentals and market behavior becomes most elastic. In these moments, markets are responding not to current conditions but to rapidly shifting beliefs about future conditions—beliefs that can change more quickly than any economic variable.

The most sophisticated investors understand this reality intuitively. George Soros's theory of reflexivity—the idea that market participants' beliefs affect the very situations they are attempting to understand—is essentially a framework for tracking the currency of confidence. Warren

Buffett's maxim to "be fearful when others are greedy and greedy when others are fearful" is a strategy for arbitraging this same currency.

For the rest of us, recognizing confidence as currency offers both warning and opportunity. The warning is that confidence, like any currency, can be debased through overuse. When confidence becomes too abundant—when it is spent too freely on increasingly speculative endeavors—its value inevitably diminishes.

The opportunity lies in developing what might be called confidence literacy—the ability to read the subtle signals of shifting collective belief before they manifest in price. This literacy involves attention to language, to behavior, to the quality of arguments, and to the treatment of dissent.

When explanations for high valuations shift from concrete to abstract, confidence may be stretching thin. When skepticism is met with ridicule rather than reasoned response, confidence may be masking insecurity. When the same evidence is used to support opposite conclusions, confidence may be seeking validation rather than truth.

These signals rarely appear on charts or in economic data. They emerge in conversations, in media coverage, in the changing tone of investor communications. They are qualitative rather than quantitative—which is precisely why they often go unnoticed until their effects become unmistakable.

As we navigate the current economic landscape, with its unprecedented monetary experiments, technological disruptions, and geopolitical uncertainties, the currency of confidence faces new tests. Artificial intelligence, like previous technological revolutions, has created legitimate excitement alongside speculative excess. The boundaries between the two are drawn not by technology itself but by the confidence invested in its promise.

The challenge for investors, policymakers, and citizens alike is to value confidence appropriately—to recognize its essential role without surrendering to its excesses. Like any currency, confidence functions best when its supply maintains a reasonable relationship to the economic activity it facilitates.

When that relationship becomes distorted—when confidence either evaporates entirely or expands beyond all reasonable proportion—markets lose their ability to allocate resources effectively. In these moments, the invisible hand that guides capitalism becomes either paralyzed by fear or intoxicated by euphoria.

The calm that precedes economic storms is often a period when confidence appears most stable while becoming increasingly brittle. The surface remains smooth even as pressures build beneath. Recognizing this pattern doesn't guarantee protection from its consequences, but it offers something perhaps more valuable: the perspective to see economic cycles not as mysterious forces beyond comprehension, but as predictable fluctuations in the currency we all trade in—the currency of collective belief.

Chapter 25: The Market as a Mirror

There is something deeply revealing about the way we build and break markets. If you stand back far enough—beyond the charts, the tickers, the endless stream of financial news—what emerges is not just an economic mechanism but a reflection of ourselves.

Markets are mirrors. They show us not what we say we value, but what we truly value. They reflect not just our rational calculations, but our hopes, fears, and deepest beliefs about the future. They capture our collective psychology in real-time, translating human emotion into price movements with startling precision.

Consider how markets respond to uncertainty. When faced with an ambiguous future, humans don't simply calculate probabilities—we tell stories. We create narratives that help us make sense of chaos. The market absorbs these narratives, amplifies them, and reflects them back to us in the language of price.

During the dot-com bubble, the market mirrored our collective wonder at the transformative potential of the internet. The soaring valuations of companies that had never turned a profit weren't just financial mistakes—they were expressions of genuine awe at a technology that promised to reshape human connection. The bubble's eventual collapse didn't invalidate the underlying transformation; it merely corrected our timeline for its economic manifestation.

Similarly, the housing crisis revealed our deep-seated beliefs about the American Dream. Home ownership wasn't just an investment—it was an identity, a status marker, a cultural touchstone. The market reflected this emotional attachment by suspending disbelief about the sustainability of endlessly rising prices. When reality finally intruded, the mirror cracked, showing us truths about ourselves we had preferred not to see.

Even in the strange case of GameStop and the meme stock phenomenon of 2021, the market served as a mirror. What appeared to financial professionals as irrational behavior was, in fact, a perfect reflection of a generation's frustration with perceived economic inequities. The market didn't malfunction—it accurately priced the value of solidarity, humor, and rebellion for a cohort of investors who ranked these qualities above traditional measures of corporate worth.

The AI boom of recent years similarly reflects our complex relationship with technology—our simultaneous hope for and fear of machines that might think like us. The massive valuations assigned to AI companies mirror our collective belief that we stand at the threshold of something profound, even if we cannot yet articulate precisely what that means for our economic future.

This mirroring function operates at multiple levels. Individual investors see their own temperaments reflected in their portfolios—the cautious in bonds, the optimistic in growth stocks, the contrarians in value plays. Societies see their values reflected in which industries attract capital—clean energy in climate-conscious eras, defense during geopolitical tension, healthcare during pandemics.

But the market as mirror shows us more than just our conscious values. It reveals our cognitive biases, our tendency toward herding, our difficulty comprehending exponential change, our preference for simple narratives over complex truths. It reflects the tension between our stated long-term goals and our actual short-term behaviors.

Perhaps most importantly, markets mirror our relationship with time itself. The discount rates we apply to future cash flows reveal our collective patience or impatience. The volatility in prices reflects our wavering confidence in what tomorrow holds. The cycles of boom and bust map perfectly to our oscillation between excessive optimism and excessive pessimism about what lies ahead.

When markets reach extreme valuations—either euphoric peaks or despairing troughs—they're showing us something important about our collective emotional state. These moments aren't failures of the market mechanism but successes of its reflecting function. They accurately capture precisely how far we've strayed from equilibrium in our thinking.

This is why the most successful investors are often those who understand that they're not just analyzing companies or economies—they're analyzing human psychology reflected through prices. Warren Buffett's famous advice to be "fearful when others are greedy and greedy when others are fearful" is an acknowledgment of the market's mirroring function and an invitation to look at the reflection with clearer eyes than the crowd.

The calm before financial storms is itself a reflection—showing us our capacity for collective denial, our preference for comfortable illusions over uncomfortable truths. The eerie stillness that precedes major market shifts reflects a moment of maximum tension between what we wish to believe and what we're beginning to suspect.

Understanding markets as mirrors offers us something valuable: the opportunity for self-reflection. When we recognize that market movements are reflecting our collective psychology, we can step back and ask whether that psychology has become distorted. We can question whether prices are reflecting fundamental realities or merely our temporary emotional relationship to those realities.

In the end, markets don't just allocate capital—they tell us who we are. They reveal our values, our temperaments, our relationship with risk, our capacity for both self-delusion and insight. They show us our tendency toward excess in both directions, and our remarkable ability to correct course, even if never as quickly as we should.

The next time you watch the market climb to dizzying heights or plunge into apparent despair, remember that you're not just witnessing an economic event. You're looking into a mirror that reflects something profound about human nature—about our eternal oscillation between fear and hope, between the desire for safety and the yearning for possibility.

And in that reflection, if we look carefully enough, we might just glimpse the approaching storm before it arrives.

Chapter 26: The Edge of Euphoria

There exists a moment in every market cycle that defies easy description—a curious psychological threshold where optimism transforms into something more potent and precarious. Economists have no precise term for it. Technical analysts might point to price charts showing parabolic moves, but these fail to capture the emotional quality of the moment. It is the edge of euphoria—that fleeting period when collective excitement reaches its zenith just before reality reasserts itself.

In the winter of 1999, you could feel it in the air in San Francisco's South of Market district. Startup employees with stock options calculated their paper wealth hourly. Conversations at bars centered not on whether someone would become a millionaire, but when. The NASDAQ had doubled in twelve months. Taxi drivers offered stock tips. College students dropped out to join companies with no revenue but soaring valuations. The physical world seemed to vibrate with possibility.

This edge of euphoria has appeared throughout history with remarkable consistency. In 1720 London, as South Sea Company shares quadrupled in months, Isaac Newton—who had initially sold his shares at a profit—watched in dismay as friends and acquaintances boasted of far greater gains. The great scientist, master of celestial mechanics and optics, surrendered to the gravitational pull of market euphoria and bought back in near the peak, eventually losing the modern equivalent of millions.

"I can calculate the movement of the stars," Newton later lamented, "but not the madness of men."

What makes this psychological state so powerful—and dangerous—is its self-reinforcing nature. As prices rise dramatically, skeptics are silenced or converted. Early caution gives way to capitulation. Those who warned of excess appear foolish as assets continue climbing. The resulting uniformity of opinion creates an environment where contrary views aren't merely rejected but become almost unthinkable.

This convergence of belief is the hallmark of the edge of euphoria. It manifests in peculiar linguistic shifts: "if" becomes "when." Contingencies disappear from conversation. The language of inevitability takes hold.

Consider the subtle transformation in how people discussed housing in 2006. "Home prices have always gone up" became the refrain, despite ample historical evidence to the contrary. In Miami and Phoenix, conversations about property no longer acknowledged risk—only the imperative to buy before being priced out forever. The conditional tense vanished from real estate discussions. The future perfect replaced it: "By next year, prices will have doubled again."

The edge of euphoria reveals itself through specific behavioral markers that transcend time and asset class. One is the proliferation of conversion stories—testimonials from former skeptics who have embraced the prevailing narrative. Another is the emergence of increasingly elaborate justifications for prices that have detached from traditional metrics. During the 2017 cryptocurrency boom, when questioned about Bitcoin's fundamental value, believers would often respond not with financial analysis but with philosophical arguments about the nature of money itself.

Perhaps most telling is the moment when participation in the boom becomes tied to personal identity. In the late 1990s, rejecting internet stocks wasn't merely seen as a financial decision but as a failure to understand the future itself. During the NFT craze of 2021, ownership of digital art became a tribal marker—a way of signaling one's membership in a forward-thinking community. The investment had transformed into something more consequential: a statement about who you were.

What makes the edge of euphoria so seductive is that, unlike the obvious mania that may follow, it often contains enough plausibility to convince rational people. The internet did indeed transform business. Housing is generally a sound long-term investment. Blockchain technology does have promising applications. The kernel of truth embedded in these movements provides intellectual cover for emotional decisions.

The temporal experience at this threshold is distinctive as well. Time seems to compress. The future rushes toward the present with increasing velocity. Long-term thinking paradoxically disappears precisely when people believe they're most focused on the future. Five-year plans collapse into five-month expectations. The horizon of possibility simultaneously expands in scope while contracting in timeframe.

In Tokyo during the late 1980s, as Japanese real estate reached such extremes that the grounds of the Imperial Palace were theoretically worth more than all of California, a strange temporal distortion took hold. Corporate executives made hundred-year business plans while simultaneously expecting stock prices to double within months. This collapse of time horizons is the cognitive signature of approaching euphoria.

What makes this phase particularly dangerous is its plausible proximity to truth. During the dot-com boom, many accurate predictions about technology's future were made—they were simply compressed into unrealistic timeframes. The internet did transform retail, but Amazon's stock price in 1999 anticipated revenues the company wouldn't achieve for nearly a decade.

The edge of euphoria is also marked by a peculiar quality of silence. Those who maintain skepticism often withdraw from conversation rather than voice contrary opinions. This creates an illusion of consensus stronger than actually exists. In private conversations during the height of the housing boom, many expressed doubts they wouldn't share publicly. This falsification of preferences—where private doubt hides behind public enthusiasm—creates a fragile edifice of apparent agreement.

The psychological weight of maintaining contrarian views becomes increasingly burdensome as euphoria builds. Michael Burry, the hedge fund manager who famously shorted the housing market before its collapse, described the immense psychological toll of maintaining his position as colleagues, investors, and the entire financial establishment insisted he was wrong. The pressure to conform doesn't just come from social circles—it emerges from within, as the mind seeks alignment with consensus to avoid cognitive dissonance.

What makes the edge of euphoria so poignant in retrospect is how it represents the last moment when collective exuberance still maintains contact with underlying reality. After this threshold is crossed, markets enter a phase where prices respond primarily to their own momentum rather than to information about the assets themselves. The connection between value and price grows increasingly tenuous until it finally, often suddenly, breaks.

History suggests we can never precisely identify this moment until after it has passed. The edge of euphoria becomes visible only in retrospect, like a watershed crossed in darkness. Yet understanding its characteristics—the compression of time, the conversion narratives, the silence of doubters, the identity markers, the philosophical justifications—offers a kind of peripheral vision. We may not see it directly, but we might sense its presence.

Perhaps the most valuable insight is recognizing that the edge of euphoria feels not like madness but like clarity. Those caught in its current often experience a sense of heightened perception—a feeling that they can see the future with unusual precision. This illusory certainty, this dissolution of doubt, is paradoxically the most reliable warning sign. When the financial future seems clearest is precisely when we should question our vision most carefully.

For in markets, as in weather, the most perfect calm often precedes the storm.

Chapter 27: Small Warnings, Soft Voices

In the months before the 1929 stock market crash, Roger Babson, an eccentric economist with a penchant for gravity-based theories of market dynamics, stood before a business conference in Massachusetts and delivered what would become known as his "crash prophecy."

"Sooner or later a crash is coming, and it may be terrific," he warned. "Factories will shut down... men will be thrown out of work... the vicious circle will get in full swing and the result will be a serious business depression."

The market dipped briefly that day—a reaction that became known as the "Babson Break"—but quickly recovered. The New York Times dismissed his concerns. The Wall Street Journal mocked him. Prominent economists called him irresponsible. Two months later, the market collapsed, initiating the Great Depression.

History does not lack for such Cassandras—those who see clearly but are destined not to be believed. Before every significant market downturn, economic crisis, or financial bubble burst, there have been voices that identified the fundamental problems, recognized the unsustainable dynamics, and attempted to sound alarms. These voices share a curious fate: they are simultaneously documented and ignored, heard but not listened to, acknowledged but dismissed.

—-

Warning signs rarely announce themselves with sirens and flashing lights. They whisper. They appear in small anomalies, subtle contradictions, and quiet inconsistencies that are easily rationalized away in the moment.

In 2006, when the housing market began showing its first cracks, the initial signals were remarkably gentle. Mortgage delinquency rates ticked up by fractions of a percentage point. Housing inventory grew slightly in previously hot markets. The rate of price appreciation slowed—not reversed, merely slowed. These were soft sounds indeed, barely audible above the continuing chorus of optimism from mortgage brokers, real estate agents, and financial institutions.

By early 2007, these whispers grew somewhat louder. HSBC announced higher-than-expected losses in its U.S. mortgage business. New Century Financial, a major subprime lender, reported accounting problems. Bear Stearns quietly began limiting investor withdrawals from mortgage-backed hedge funds. Each event was treated as isolated, specific to a particular company or segment, rather than connected symptoms of a systemic disease.

Even as these warnings accumulated, Federal Reserve Chairman Ben Bernanke assured Congress that subprime problems were "contained" and would not seriously harm the broader economy. Treasury Secretary Henry Paulson declared the housing correction "largely behind us." These were not statements of deliberate deception but reflections of a collective inability to integrate disconfirming evidence into the prevailing narrative.

—-

The phenomenon extends beyond financial markets. The history of corporate collapses, from Enron to Theranos, reveals a similar pattern of ignored warnings. Enron's implosion was preceded by years of questions from short sellers and analysts about its opaque accounting practices. Theranos had former employees, medical professionals, and journalists raising concerns about its technology long before its final unraveling.

The pattern is consistent: the warnings begin as technical concerns from specialists with deep domain expertise. They are dismissed as overly complex, unnecessarily pessimistic, or motivated by self-interest. As problems grow more evident, the warnings expand beyond specialists to more visible figures, but by then, too many reputations and fortunes are invested in maintaining the status quo.

Why do these small warnings go unheeded? The answer lies not in a failure of information but in the human capacity for selective attention and collective reinforcement.

First, warnings often come from those positioned at the edges of systems—academics without "real world" experience, newcomers who haven't been properly socialized, or outsiders without institutional credibility. Their structural position makes them easier to dismiss.

Second, warnings frequently involve complex, technical details that don't translate easily into compelling narratives. The problems with collateralized debt obligations in 2007 required understanding tranches, default correlations, and rating methodologies—concepts that resisted simple explanation compared to the straightforward story of ever-rising home values.

Third, and perhaps most importantly, warnings challenge not just ideas but identities. To acknowledge a warning is to admit that one's prior judgments, decisions, and beliefs may have been mistaken. This threatens not only financial positions but also professional reputations and self-conceptions.

—-

The dynamics of ignored warnings reveal something profound about how we collectively process information. We do not simply evaluate data on its merits; we filter it through existing beliefs, social consensus, and institutional incentives.

Consider how warnings are typically received in the late stages of a market bubble. The initial response is dismissal: *This person doesn't understand the new paradigm.* As evidence mounts, the response shifts to minimization: *The concerns are valid but exaggerated.* When problems become undeniable, the response becomes temporal distancing: *Yes, there will eventually be a correction, but not anytime soon.*

Only after the bubble bursts does the final stage arrive: revisionist acceptance, where everyone claims they saw the problems all along. The warnings that were ignored become, in retrospect, "obvious" signs that "everyone" should have recognized.

This pattern played out with remarkable consistency during the dot-com bubble, the housing crisis, and the cryptocurrency boom. The specific assets changed, but the human response to warnings remained constant.

—-

What makes certain warnings penetrate this defensive perimeter while others fail? The rare warnings that gain traction typically share several characteristics.

They come from insiders with established credibility—people who cannot easily be dismissed as uninformed outsiders. They present concerns in concrete, vivid terms rather than abstract possibilities. They acknowledge uncertainty while still conveying urgency. Perhaps most crucially, they frame the warning not as a rebuke of past decisions but as an opportunity to make better future ones, allowing people to change course without losing face.

Warren Buffett's famous warning about derivatives as "financial weapons of mass destruction" gained traction because it came from a respected market participant, used vivid imagery, and was delivered without suggesting that those involved in derivatives were foolish or corrupt—merely that they were dealing with instruments whose risks were not fully understood.

But even the most perfectly crafted warnings face an uphill battle against what psychologists call the "normalcy bias"—our tendency to assume that things will continue as they have been, even in the face of evidence to the contrary.

—

As I write these words, new warnings are being sounded about various aspects of our financial system: the sustainability of corporate debt levels, the concentration of stock market gains in a handful of technology companies, the potential fragility of passive investment vehicles during a serious downturn, the hidden leverage in private equity, and the unknown consequences of unwinding years of extraordinary monetary policy.

Some of these warnings will prove prescient; others will not. The challenge is not simply to identify which warnings to heed—an impossible task with certainty—but to create systems and cultures that process warnings more effectively, that can hear the soft voices before they are forced to become screams.

This requires institutional mechanisms that reward rather than punish those who identify potential problems. It demands intellectual frameworks that can integrate contradictory information rather than simply filtering it out. Most fundamentally, it calls for a relationship with uncertainty that allows us to hold provisional beliefs rather than hardened convictions.

The soft voices of warning will always be with us, whispering from the periphery of our attention. The question is whether we can develop the capacity to listen—not with uncritical acceptance of every dire prediction, but with an openness to signals that might contradict our preferred narratives. For in that listening lies not just the possibility of avoiding catastrophe, but of understanding more deeply the complex systems we have created and our place within them.

The warnings are there. They always have been. The stillness before the storm is rarely silent for those willing to hear.

Chapter 28: Pressure Hidden in the System

There is a peculiar quality to the way pressure accumulates in complex systems. Unlike the visible strain of a dam holding back water or the audible creaking of ice about to fracture, financial pressure builds in silence, distributed across countless invisible connections. The most dangerous accumulations of systemic risk are rarely where we are looking.

In the summer of 2007, economists at major financial institutions were still debating whether the growing problems in subprime mortgages represented a contained risk or something more serious. The prevailing view was containment. After all, subprime represented only about 13 percent of the total mortgage market. How could trouble in such a relatively small sector threaten the entire global financial system?

What this analysis missed was not the visible risk, but the hidden connections—the complex web of dependencies that had been constructed around these mortgages. The pressure wasn't just in the mortgages themselves but in the elaborate financial architecture built upon them: the collateralized debt obligations, the credit default swaps, the special investment vehicles kept off balance sheets, and the implicit guarantees that existed between institutions.

"Complex systems fail in complex ways," wrote Richard Cook in his studies of how catastrophic failures occur. Financial systems are perhaps the most intricate human constructions, with layers of abstraction built upon other layers of abstraction. When we speak of "pressure in the system," we're describing something that exists primarily in the spaces between—in the relationships, expectations, and dependencies that connect different parts of the whole.

Consider how pressure manifested in the weeks before the 2008 crisis fully erupted. Bear Stearns hadn't yet failed. Lehman Brothers still appeared solvent. But the interbank lending market—where financial institutions lend to one another overnight—had begun to freeze. This wasn't visible to ordinary observers. It wasn't even fully understood by many inside the system. But this tightening of credit between institutions that supposedly trusted one another was the pressure gauge flashing red.

The most telling indicator wasn't any single data point but a change in behavior: banks that had routinely lent to each other for decades were suddenly demanding higher collateral or refusing to lend at all. Trust, that invisible foundation of finance, was eroding before any major institution had actually collapsed.

This pattern repeats across history. Before the crash of 1929, the pressure wasn't most evident in stock prices but in the margin lending that supported them. Before the collapse of Long-Term Capital Management in 1998, the danger wasn't in their trading strategies but in how those strategies were financed and the implicit assumption that markets would remain liquid enough to exit positions if needed.

Our financial instruments have grown more sophisticated, but our ability to see the connections between them has not kept pace. We've built financial MRI machines that can examine individual assets with extraordinary precision, but we lack the equivalent of full-body scans that might reveal how stress in one area affects the whole.

The most concerning pressures in our current system may be similarly hidden from view. They might exist in the leverage embedded in private equity, the duration mismatch in bond portfolios, the concentration of assets in passive investment vehicles, or the liquidity assumptions underlying complex derivatives. Or perhaps in something we're not discussing at all.

What makes these hidden pressures so dangerous is not just their invisibility but how they interact with human psychology. When pressure builds gradually, we adjust our perception of normal. The frog in slowly heating water doesn't jump out—not because it can't, but because the incremental change doesn't trigger its threat response. Similarly, financial systems adapt to slowly building pressure, recalibrating risk models and adjusting expectations until what would have once seemed dangerous becomes the new baseline.

This psychological adaptation explains why warnings often go unheeded. Those who point to building pressure are dismissed as alarmists because the system appears to be functioning normally. The very absence of visible crisis becomes evidence that no crisis looms. Yet history shows that systems often appear most stable just before they fail.

In engineering, there's a concept called "graceful degradation"—the idea that well-designed systems should fail in predictable, manageable ways. Financial systems, despite their sophistication, rarely degrade gracefully. Instead, they exhibit what engineers call "tight coupling," where failure in one component rapidly affects others, creating cascading effects that quickly overwhelm safeguards.

The most dangerous aspect of hidden pressure is not that it exists—all systems contain stress—but that we systematically underestimate how quickly it can transform from chronic to acute. Markets that have functioned smoothly for years can seize up in days. Liquidity that seemed abundant can vanish overnight. Correlations that statistical models assured us were impossible suddenly become reality.

Perhaps the most subtle form of pressure building in today's system is cognitive. After years of central bank intervention following the 2008 crisis, market participants have internalized the belief that authorities will prevent any significant downturn—the so-called "Fed put." This belief has changed risk calculations across the financial landscape, encouraging behavior that might otherwise seem imprudent.

Yet this confidence itself creates pressure. It leads to greater risk-taking, more leverage, and less caution—all predicated on the assumption that the system as a whole is protected. The irony is that the very belief in system stability may be making the system less stable, creating pressure that remains invisible until it suddenly isn't.

As we navigate the current economic landscape, with its unprecedented monetary policies, technological disruptions, and geopolitical tensions, we would do well to remember that the most significant risks are rarely where the spotlight shines brightest. They lurk in the assumptions we've stopped questioning, in the correlations we believe will hold forever, and in the dependencies we've forgotten exist.

The pressure hidden in the system isn't a reason for panic. It's a call for humility—a reminder that our financial models, no matter how sophisticated, are simplifications of a reality too complex to fully capture. And it's an invitation to look beyond the obvious, to question comfortable assumptions, and to remember that in complex systems, stability itself can be deceptive.

The storm, when it comes, rarely arrives from the direction we're watching.

Chapter 29: When the Music Stops

There is a peculiar silence that falls across a room when music suddenly ceases. For a moment, conversations hang suspended in air, dancers freeze mid-step, and everyone seems to hold their breath, waiting. This fleeting instant—between the end of one song and the beginning of another—reveals the scaffolding beneath our social rituals, exposing the constructed nature of the moment we had, just seconds before, accepted as reality.

Financial markets experience similar moments of suspended animation.

In July 2007, Chuck Prince, then CEO of Citigroup, offered what would become one of the most infamous quotes in financial history: "As long as the music is playing, you've got to get up and dance." Three months later, Citigroup announced write-downs of $8.9 billion in subprime-related losses, and Prince resigned. The music had stopped, but the dancers couldn't leave the floor.

What happens in these pivotal moments when financial rhythms falter? The transition from confidence to doubt occurs with a peculiar grammar all its own—not the dramatic crash we might expect, but something more nuanced and human.

The first sign is often silence itself.

Markets don't immediately collapse when sentiment shifts. Instead, there's a strange pause—trading volumes decline, deals slow, and a watchful quietude descends. This isn't the tranquility of stability but the stillness of collective assessment. Like diners who've just heard a strange sound from the kitchen, market participants pause their conversations to listen.

In August 1929, two months before the crash, trading volume on the New York Stock Exchange mysteriously contracted. In early 2000, before the dot-com collapse, venture capital quietly began withholding follow-on funding from less promising startups. In mid-2007, mortgage originators discreetly tightened lending standards. These were not dramatic events that made headlines—they were subtle shifts in rhythm, noticeable only to those paying careful attention.

The second sign is the sudden visibility of exits.

During periods of market euphoria, few concern themselves with how they might eventually sell their assets. The assumption of perpetual liquidity—that there will always be a buyer at a reasonable price—becomes an article of faith. But when sentiment shifts, exits suddenly become conspicuous by their narrowing. The question "How will I sell this?" emerges from the background into sharp focus.

This realization doesn't strike all participants simultaneously. It begins at the margins, with the most sophisticated or most leveraged players quietly moving toward the doors. Their movements create small disturbances in price and liquidity that most dismiss as temporary. The broader market continues its dance, perhaps with slightly less enthusiasm, while a few participants have already taken their coats from the cloakroom.

The third sign is the changing nature of conversation.

Market narratives don't collapse all at once—they erode. The language shifts subtly from certainty to contingency. "This will happen" becomes "this should happen." Phrases like "assuming conditions remain favorable" begin to appear in analyst reports. Questions that would have seemed absurd weeks earlier are suddenly entertained as reasonable.

During this phase, we witness what sociologists call "preference falsification"—people continue to publicly express confidence while privately harboring doubts. This creates an unstable equilibrium where market sentiment appears stronger than it actually is. Everyone is watching everyone else for signs of wavering conviction.

The most dangerous moment arrives when uncertainty itself becomes contagious.

Financial markets can accommodate many things—bad news, high prices, even irrational exuberance. What they cannot tolerate is fundamental uncertainty about the rules of the game. When participants begin questioning not just asset prices but the integrity of the market mechanism itself, the music truly stops.

This occurred in September 2008 when Lehman Brothers failed. The question shifted from "Which institutions are solvent?" to "Can we trust counterparty relationships at all?" Money market funds, the most conservative investment vehicles, suddenly seemed risky. The commercial paper market—the mundane financial plumbing that keeps corporations functioning day-to-day—froze entirely.

What makes these transitions so dangerous is that they reveal the inherent circularity of financial confidence. Markets function because we collectively believe they function. When that belief wavers, the self-reinforcing cycle that once pushed prices upward begins working in reverse.

Consider how quickly sentiment shifted during the 2008 crisis. In March, Bear Stearns required emergency intervention. By September, Lehman Brothers failed. By October, even the strongest banks needed capital injections from the government. The progression wasn't linear—it was exponential, accelerating as each failure undermined confidence in the system itself.

The human element in these transitions cannot be overstated.

Financial models struggle to capture these inflection points precisely because they're fundamentally social phenomena. The shift from confidence to doubt doesn't occur because of a specific economic threshold being crossed, but because of a change in how we collectively interpret information.

During the 2000 dot-com crash, the fundamental economics of internet companies hadn't suddenly deteriorated—what changed was the lens through which investors viewed those same facts. Losses that had once been interpreted as "investment in growth" were suddenly seen as "unsustainable cash burn." Same facts, different frame.

This interpretive shift explains why market transitions often feel like awakening from a collective dream. The new perspective doesn't just change our view of the present—it retroactively transforms our understanding of the past. "How did we not see this coming?" becomes the common refrain, even among those who were most confident just months earlier.

The most poignant aspect of these transitions is their inevitability.

Every market cycle contains the seeds of its own reversal. The longer stability persists, the more participants come to depend on its continuation. Strategies adapt to prevailing conditions, leverage increases, caution diminishes. The very success of the system changes behavior in ways that ultimately undermine that system.

This doesn't mean markets are fundamentally irrational—only that they're human. They reflect our tendency to extrapolate from recent experience, our social nature, and our limited capacity to maintain vigilance during extended periods of calm.

When the music finally stops, the silence isn't just the absence of noise—it's the sound of recognition. It's the collective realization that what we believed was a permanent state was actually a temporary condition. The dancers don't immediately leave the floor; they stand in place, suddenly aware of their position, wondering what comes next.

And in that moment of suspended animation—between the end of one financial rhythm and the beginning of another—we glimpse something essential about markets and ourselves: the fragile, contingent nature of confidence, and how quickly certainty can dissolve into doubt.

The question then becomes not if the music will start again, but when, and what melody it will play.

Chapter 30: The Avalanche That Starts With a Whisper

The most dangerous moments in financial history often begin not with a thunderclap, but with a whisper.

In the winter of 1637, in a tavern in Haarlem, a Dutch merchant quietly declined to bid on a Semper Augustus tulip bulb for the first time in months. The auctioneer paused, waiting for the familiar rhythm of escalating bids. The room held its breath. Someone coughed. The price was lowered slightly. Still, no hands raised. What happened in that room—that small hesitation, that first moment of collective doubt—would cascade through the Dutch Republic in the days that followed, collapsing the world's first documented speculative bubble.

Financial avalanches begin this way: not with dramatic proclamations or front-page headlines, but with subtle shifts in confidence that spread person to person, institution to institution, like a contagion seeking hosts.

Consider how the 2008 financial crisis truly began. Not with the bankruptcy of Lehman Brothers—that was merely the moment when the avalanche became visible to all. The first whispers came months earlier, in the summer of 2007, when two Bear Stearns hedge funds quietly imploded. Their failure received modest coverage, dismissed as an isolated event affecting only sophisticated investors who understood the risks they were taking.

"The subprime mortgage difficulties are likely to be contained," said Federal Reserve Chairman Ben Bernanke in March 2007, words that would later haunt him.

What followed was not a sudden collapse but a slow-motion avalanche, gathering momentum with each passing week. BNP Paribas froze three investment funds in August 2007, unable to value their mortgage holdings. Northern Rock experienced Britain's first bank run in over a century the following month. Each event was rationalized, compartmentalized, explained away—until explanation became impossible.

The metaphor of an avalanche is particularly apt. Snow accumulates gradually on a mountainside, building pressure invisibly. Then a small disturbance—perhaps nothing more than the echo of a distant voice—dislodges a handful of snow. This minor shift redistributes weight, causing another small section to give way. Each movement triggers another, slightly larger one, until the entire snowpack is in motion. What begins as a whisper ends as a roar.

Financial markets operate with similar physics. The system absorbs pressure over time—excessive leverage, deteriorating loan quality, concentrated risk—while appearing stable on the surface. The triggering event itself is rarely significant enough to justify what follows. It is merely the final snowflake that reveals the structural instability that was there all along.

In October 1929, the whisper came when a handful of large investors began quietly liquidating positions. The market had already peaked on September 3, but most investors remained confident. When prices began falling on Thursday, October 24, the initial reaction was to buy the dip, as we would say today. Leading bankers met at J.P. Morgan's offices and pledged to support the market. Richard Whitney, vice president of the New York Stock Exchange, made a show of placing large buy orders for blue-chip stocks. The market stabilized briefly.

But the whisper had already started the avalanche. By Monday, the selling pressure overwhelmed all attempts at intervention. Tuesday brought "Black Tuesday," when the Dow Jones Industrial Average fell nearly 12 percent in a single day. The Great Crash had arrived.

What makes these whispers so potent is that financial markets are, at their core, elaborate consensus mechanisms. Prices reflect not economic reality but our collective beliefs about economic reality.

When those beliefs begin to shift, even subtly, the foundation of the market shifts with them.

The digital age has both amplified these whispers and accelerated their spread. In 2010, the "Flash Crash" saw the Dow Jones plummet nearly 1,000 points in minutes before recovering most of its losses. The initial trigger? A large sell order executed by a mutual fund in Kansas City, which algorithmic trading systems misinterpreted and amplified into a cascade of selling.

More recently, in March 2023, the collapse of Silicon Valley Bank demonstrated how quickly whispers become shouts in our interconnected world. What began as concerns about the bank's bond portfolio shared among venture capitalists on private messaging platforms transformed within 48 hours into the second-largest bank failure in American history. By the time CNBC and Bloomberg were reporting the story, the bank run was already well underway, orchestrated through text messages and Slack channels.

"We are witnessing the first Twitter-fueled bank run," wrote one financial analyst as the crisis unfolded.

The whispers that start financial avalanches often contain a kernel of truth. Silicon Valley Bank did have unrealized losses in its bond portfolio. Mortgage-backed securities in 2007 were indeed declining in value. The Dutch tulip market of 1637 had reached unsustainable prices. The whisper does not create the vulnerability—it merely reveals it.

This pattern appears with such consistency across financial history that we might wonder why we remain so vulnerable to it. The answer lies partly in our psychological makeup. We are social creatures who take cues from those around us. When we see others growing concerned, we naturally question our own confidence. This is rational at the individual level but potentially catastrophic at the collective level.

There is also an inherent asymmetry in financial decision-making: the cost of overreacting to a false alarm can be measured in foregone profits, but the cost of underreacting to a genuine crisis can be financial ruin. When uncertainty rises, the rational response is to reduce exposure—to move to safety until the situation clarifies. When many market participants make this same calculation simultaneously, liquidity evaporates precisely when it is most needed.

Some whispers, of course, remain just that—concerns that never materialize into crises. In 2011, many expected a European sovereign debt crisis to trigger a global financial collapse. In 2016, the Brexit vote was predicted to cause immediate economic calamity. In 2018, rising interest rates were widely expected to end the bull market. Each time, markets absorbed the shock and continued.

The challenge for investors, policymakers, and citizens alike is discerning which whispers presage avalanches and which are merely background noise. There is no perfect formula for this distinction, but there are patterns worth noting.

Whispers that spread most rapidly tend to touch on fundamental beliefs that support market valuations. In the housing crisis, the whisper challenged the belief that nationwide home prices could not decline simultaneously. In the dot-com crash, it questioned whether companies without profits could justify billion-dollar valuations. In each case, once the foundational narrative began to crack, the entire structure became unstable.

The most dangerous whispers are those that create what economist Hyman Minsky called "Ponzi units" in the financial system—investments that can only succeed if asset prices continue rising. When the whisper suggests that the rise might pause or reverse, the mathematical inevitability of collapse becomes apparent to those who understand the structure.

Perhaps most importantly, whispers gain power when they align with what many already suspect but have been unwilling to acknowledge publicly. The most effective whispers don't introduce entirely new information—they crystallize existing doubts that have been suppressed by social consensus.

This is why markets can appear so resilient until they suddenly aren't. The façade of confidence can remain intact even as doubts multiply beneath the surface. We maintain the pretense of certainty because everyone else seems certain, creating a fragile equilibrium that can shatter with a single whisper that gives others permission to voice their private concerns.

The whisper that starts an avalanche is rarely recorded for posterity. It happens in private conversations, in subtle shifts of positioning, in the growing hesitation before making new commitments. By the time the avalanche is visible to all, its origins have been obscured by the scale of what follows.

Yet understanding this pattern offers a kind of preparation, if not prediction. It teaches us to listen more carefully to the quiet conversations happening at the margins of consensus. It reminds us that stability itself can become a source of instability when it leads to complacency and excess. And it suggests that the most important signals may be the ones that are hardest to hear—the subtle shifts in tone that precede the roar.

In the calm before the storm, the wise listener attends not to what is being shouted from the center, but to what is being whispered at the edges. For it is there, in those barely audible concerns, that we might discern the first tremors of the avalanche to come.

Chapter 31: Panic as Contagion

When panic arrives in financial markets, it doesn't spread like wildfire—that metaphor is too simple, too visible. It moves like an airborne pathogen: invisible, exponential, and following networks of connection we didn't fully map until they were carrying the contagion.

In March 2020, as the world confronted a literal pandemic, financial markets demonstrated their own version of contagion mechanics. The Dow Jones Industrial Average fell 2,997 points in a single day—the largest point drop in history. What began as concern about specific sectors directly affected by lockdowns quickly infected every corner of the market. Oil prices, corporate bonds, commercial real estate, currencies—all succumbed to the same psychological virus: fear.

But this pattern isn't unique to pandemic-era markets. It is the standard transmission mechanism of financial panic.

Consider how differently humans process information during periods of calm versus periods of stress. When markets appear stable, we evaluate assets individually, distinguishing between the promising and the problematic. We make fine distinctions. We see nuance. During panic, however, these cognitive habits dissolve. Everything becomes correlated. Assets that have nothing fundamentally in common suddenly move in lockstep, as if controlled by the same invisible hand.

"In a crisis, all correlations go to one," said David Viniar, then-CFO of Goldman Sachs during the 2008 financial crisis. This observation captures something profound about financial contagion. When panic takes hold, the market stops seeing individual securities and starts seeing only risk itself.

The psychology behind this phenomenon runs deeper than simple fear. It involves a fundamental reassessment of reality itself.

During the 1907 financial panic, rumors began circulating about the solvency of the Knickerbocker Trust Company. Within days, depositors formed lines outside the bank's doors, each person's anxiety visibly reinforcing the next person's. By October 22, the bank had paid out $8 million to frightened depositors before finally closing its doors. The sight of those closed doors then triggered runs on other banks throughout New York.

What's striking about this episode—and countless others like it—is how the panic spread not just through financial connections but through social and psychological ones. Each person in line outside Knickerbocker served as both victim and vector of the contagion.

We see this same pattern in digital form during modern market panics. In 2008, as Lehman Brothers collapsed, the fear didn't remain contained to investment banks. It leapt across previously unconnected markets: commercial paper, money market funds, commodities, even consumer goods. The connections weren't obvious until the panic revealed them.

The financial system, for all its mathematical sophistication, remains a human system. And humans are social creatures who take their cues from one another. When we see others running, our instinct is not to carefully assess whether their fear is rational—it's to run alongside them.

This is why market panics accelerate rather than proceed at a steady pace. Each new participant in the panic adds to the social proof that danger exists. The system becomes self-reinforcing.

In 1997, as the Asian Financial Crisis unfolded, international investors initially viewed Thailand's currency problems as isolated. Within months, however, the contagion had spread to Indonesia, South Korea, Hong Kong, and other seemingly unrelated economies. What connected these markets wasn't just economic fundamentals but the psychology of the investors themselves, who began to question all emerging markets once one showed weakness.

The digital age has only accelerated these contagion mechanisms. Information—and misinformation—now travels at the speed of light rather than the speed of gossip. When Silicon Valley Bank collapsed in 2023, the bank run that precipitated its fall happened largely through smartphone screens and social media platforms. Depositors didn't need to see physical lines outside the bank; the virtual panic was enough.

What makes financial contagion particularly dangerous is that it creates its own reality. A bank that might have remained solvent in the absence of a panic becomes insolvent precisely because of the panic. The fear becomes self-fulfilling.

This dynamic reveals something crucial about financial markets: they are not just mechanisms for price discovery but also for confidence discovery. When confidence breaks, prices follow—often in ways that seem to defy rational explanation.

During the most severe phases of market contagion, we witness what psychologists call "emotional contagion"—the literal transmission of feeling states from one person to another. Studies of trading floors during crisis periods show that emotional states spread between traders through facial expressions, body language, and vocal tones, even before any words are exchanged about market conditions.

The contagion doesn't just spread between individuals but between markets themselves. In 2011, as the European sovereign debt crisis intensified, yields on Italian government bonds rose sharply after Greece revealed the true extent of its fiscal problems. There was no direct mechanical connection—Italy's debt situation was fundamentally different from Greece's—but the psychological connection was enough.

What begins as rational reassessment quickly becomes something more primal. The human brain, when confronted with perceived threats, shifts processing from the prefrontal cortex (responsible for complex analysis) to the amygdala (responsible for fight-or-flight responses). This neurological shift helps explain why market panics often seem to bypass rational thought.

The most dangerous form of financial contagion occurs when the panic jumps from financial markets to the real economy. When businesses suddenly cannot access credit, when consumers abruptly stop spending, when employers freeze hiring—these are moments when the psychological virus escapes the financial system and infects the broader economy.

This is what made the Great Depression so devastating. What began as a stock market crash in 1929 spread to the banking system, then to business investment, then to consumer spending, then to employment. Each step in this contagion chain amplified the previous one.

The metaphor of contagion is not merely poetic—it offers practical insights. Just as public health officials study disease transmission to prevent pandemics, financial regulators must understand the networks through which panic spreads to prevent financial crises.

After each major financial crisis, regulators typically focus on addressing the specific vulnerabilities that triggered that particular panic. But this approach misses the broader pattern: financial contagion will always find the path of least resistance. The next crisis rarely looks exactly like the last one.

What remains constant is not the specific trigger but the transmission mechanism—the way human psychology transforms isolated concerns into systemic ones. Understanding this mechanism doesn't just help us prepare for crises; it helps us recognize when we're in the early stages of one.

The quiet that precedes financial storms—that strange stillness we explored at the beginning of this book—eventually gives way to its opposite: the roaring panic that seems to engulf everything at once. But between these extremes lies a critical transition period when the contagion is just beginning to spread, when containment might still be possible.

This is why the most valuable skill in financial markets might not be valuation or technical analysis, but rather the ability to detect the first subtle signs of contagion—before the pandemic of panic has declared itself.

Chapter 32: The Blame That Comes Too Late

In the aftermath of financial collapse, there comes a peculiar season of blame. It arrives like winter after autumn—inevitable, clarifying, and much too late to save the harvest.

The morning after Lehman Brothers collapsed in September 2008, the financial pages transformed. The same publications that had celebrated the housing boom's architects now scrutinized them with surgical precision. The same television programs that had featured house-flipping success stories now hosted solemn panels dissecting regulatory failure. The same politicians who had championed financial deregulation now called for accountability with righteous indignation.

This pattern of delayed blame is as predictable as the crisis cycle itself.

Consider the congressional hearings that followed the 1929 crash. For weeks, the nation watched as financial titans were summoned before elected officials. The public spectacle provided catharsis but little insight. The most revealing moment came when Richard Whitney, president of the New York Stock Exchange, was asked about the market's collapse. "The Exchange," he testified with perfect composure, "is a perfect institution."

Five years later, Whitney would be convicted of embezzlement and sent to Sing Sing prison. The irony was lost on no one.

The blame that follows financial crisis serves many purposes, few of them constructive. It satisfies our need for narrative closure—every story requires its villain. It absolves the collective of responsibility by focusing attention on individual actors. Most importantly, it creates the comforting illusion that if only these particular people had been stopped, or these specific regulations enacted, catastrophe could have been averted.

This is rarely true.

After the dot-com bubble burst, analysts blamed unscrupulous tech CEOs and their venture capital enablers. After 2008, blame centered on predatory mortgage lenders, reckless investment banks, and captured regulators. After the meme stock frenzy collapsed, attention turned to social media influencers and gamified trading platforms. Each narrative contained elements of truth while missing the broader pattern.

The uncomfortable reality is that financial crises rarely result from the actions of a few bad actors. They emerge from systems operating exactly as designed, pushed to their logical conclusion. The same incentives that produce growth during boom times inevitably produce excess when left unchecked. The same psychological tendencies that create market efficiency in normal times create market delusion at extremes.

This is why the blame that comes after crisis feels both satisfying and hollow. It identifies proximate causes while overlooking ultimate ones.

Consider the ritual of congressional testimony. After each major financial collapse, senior executives are summoned before committees. They arrive in conservative suits, speak in measured tones, and offer carefully crafted apologies that acknowledge mistakes without admitting liability. Lawmakers alternate between performative outrage and technical questions clearly prepared by staff. The public watches, momentarily satisfied that accountability is being served.

But what changes? After the savings and loan crisis of the 1980s, after the Long-Term Capital Management collapse, after the dot-com implosion, after the housing crisis—each time, the fundamental structures remained largely intact. The players changed; the game did not.

The anthropologist Mary Douglas once observed that blame is primarily a mechanism for reinforcing social boundaries—for determining who belongs within the circle of trust and who stands outside it. Financial blame-casting serves this function perfectly. By identifying and punishing selected transgressors, we reaffirm our collective values while avoiding more difficult questions about those values themselves.

The timing of blame also matters. It arrives after the damage is done, when clarity is cheap. During the buildup to crisis—when intervention might actually prevent collapse—those who question the prevailing narrative are rarely celebrated. They are dismissed as pessimists, doom-mongers, or simply people who "don't get it."

Cassandra, in Greek mythology, was cursed to speak true prophecies that no one would believe. Every financial cycle produces its Cassandras: Brooksley Born warning about unregulated derivatives before the 2008 crash; Robert Shiller questioning housing valuations while prices still soared; Michael Burry identifying mortgage securities' fundamental flaws while markets still cheered them on.

We remember these figures in retrospect, forgetting how thoroughly they were marginalized in real time. Their vindication comes too late to matter—except as characters in books and films created years after the collapse they foresaw.

There is something almost ceremonial about our post-crisis blame rituals. They follow a prescribed sequence: initial shock gives way to anger; anger demands targets; targets are identified and subjected to public scrutiny; scrutiny produces superficial reforms; reforms create the impression of resolution; resolution allows the cycle to begin again.

This is not to suggest that accountability is meaningless. When laws are broken, consequences should follow. When trust is violated, restoration requires acknowledgment. But true accountability would require something more difficult: examining not just who broke the rules, but whether the rules themselves—both formal and informal—create the conditions for crisis.

The most profound failure of post-crisis blame is its selective memory. We focus intensely on those who committed the most egregious excesses while forgetting our own participation. Few homeowners during the housing boom questioned rising valuations. Few retail investors during the dot-com bubble questioned business models without profits. Few cryptocurrency enthusiasts questioned the fundamental value of digital assets with no underlying utility.

We were all, in small ways, contributors to the collective delusion. This is what makes financial bubbles possible—not just the greed of a few, but the hope and credulity of many.

Perhaps the most honest response to financial collapse came from Chuck Prince, the former CEO of Citigroup. Asked why his bank continued providing risky loans as the housing market showed signs of stress, he famously replied: "As long as the music is playing, you've got to get up and dance." The statement was widely condemned as evidence of recklessness, but it contained an uncomfortable truth: individual actors within a system rarely have the incentive or ability to resist its momentum.

The blame that comes after crisis satisfies our need for justice without addressing this fundamental reality. It provides the comforting fiction that next time will be different because we've identified and punished those responsible. It allows us to believe that the storm was an anomaly rather than an inevitable feature of the weather.

True understanding would require something more difficult: recognizing that financial crises emerge from the same human tendencies that drive progress—our optimism, our social nature, our capacity for narrative, our ability to imagine futures different from the present. The same qualities that build markets can, in excess, undermine them.

This is why the blame that comes too late feels both necessary and insufficient. It closes one chapter without truly opening the next. It allows us to move forward without looking too deeply at where we've been or where we're going.

And so the cycle continues, with each generation convinced it has learned the lessons of the past, each boom accompanied by new narratives of permanent prosperity, each bust followed by its season of blame—arriving, as always, when the damage is already done.

Chapter 33: The Long Work of Rebuilding Trust

In the aftermath of financial collapse, the landscape resembles a city after an earthquake. The physical structures may still stand—banks maintain their marble facades, stock exchanges their digital screens, regulators their offices—but the invisible architecture of trust that allows these institutions to function lies in ruins. This chapter is not about the immediate emergency response that follows crisis, but about the slower, more difficult work that comes after: the rebuilding of trust.

Trust is the essential yet invisible infrastructure of finance. Like clean water flowing through underground pipes, we notice it only when it vanishes. When present, it allows capital to move efficiently, enables strangers to trade with confidence, and permits us to plan beyond the immediate future. When broken, even the simplest financial transactions become fraught with suspicion and hesitation.

Consider what happened after 2008. The mechanics of markets were restored relatively quickly—trading resumed, interest rates were slashed, emergency liquidity flooded the system. But the deeper damage lingered. A 2012 Gallup poll showed that only 21 percent of Americans had confidence in banks, down from 41 percent before the crisis. Similar erosions of trust appeared in institutions ranging from Congress to corporations to the Federal Reserve. This wasn't merely public relations damage; it represented a fundamental tear in the social contract.

The rebuilding process follows patterns we can observe across history. After the Panic of 1907, it took the creation of the Federal Reserve in 1913 to restore confidence in America's banking system. Following the Great Depression, the Glass-Steagall Act, the Securities and Exchange Commission, and deposit insurance formed a new foundation of trust that would last for decades. After the Savings and

Loan Crisis of the 1980s, regulatory reforms and prosecutions served as public demonstrations that the system could correct itself.

Yet there is something different about our modern cycles of trust restoration. The work seems to grow more difficult with each crisis, the recovery of confidence more tenuous. Perhaps this is because we are now witnessing not just the aftermath of isolated financial events, but the cumulative effect of repeated breaches of trust across multiple domains—political, technological, environmental, and financial.

The process of rebuilding trust after crisis follows distinct phases that we can trace across centuries of financial history:

First comes transparency—the opening of books, the disclosure of losses, the acknowledgment of mistakes. This is often resisted initially, as institutions fear that revealing the full extent of damage will only deepen the crisis. Yet history shows that attempted concealment prolongs rather than shortens the recovery period. Japan's "lost decade" following its banking crisis in the 1990s offers a stark lesson in how delayed recognition of losses can extend economic suffering.

"The first step toward rebuilding trust is not reassurance," explained former Federal Reserve Chairman Paul Volcker in 2009. "It's honesty about how bad things really are."

The second phase involves accountability—determining who was responsible and ensuring appropriate consequences. This isn't merely punitive; it serves as a public demonstration that the system can identify and correct its own failings. After the 2008 crisis, the relative absence of high-profile prosecutions—especially when contrasted with the hundreds of bankers jailed after the Savings and Loan Crisis—left a lingering sense that accountability remained incomplete.

The third phase involves structural reform—changing the rules, incentives, and institutions to prevent similar failures. The Dodd-Frank Act of 2010 represented an attempt at such reform, introducing stress tests for banks, the Consumer Financial Protection Bureau, and restrictions on proprietary trading. Yet the effectiveness of these reforms remains debated, and many were subsequently weakened or reversed—a common pattern in the decades following crises, as memory fades and lobbying intensifies.

The final and most elusive phase is cultural change—shifting the values, priorities, and assumptions that guide financial decision-making. This is where reform efforts most often fall short. Regulatory changes can alter behavior temporarily, but lasting change requires a deeper shift in what we collectively value and reward.

Consider how differently this process unfolded after the Great Depression versus after 2008. The reforms of the 1930s were accompanied by a profound cultural reassessment of capitalism itself. Financial restraint became a virtue, speculation was viewed with suspicion, and a generation internalized lessons about risk that would shape their behavior for decades. After 2008, despite similar initial outrage, the cultural reset was more muted. By 2015, surveys showed that financial sector practices had changed less than reformers had hoped, and public attention had largely moved on.

Why is rebuilding trust so difficult in our modern context? Several factors complicate the process.

First, the increasing complexity of finance makes transparency more challenging. When J.P. Morgan personally intervened to halt the Panic of 1907, the mechanics of his solution could be understood by most educated citizens. Today's financial system, with its collateralized debt obligations, algorithmic trading, and global interconnections, resists simple explanation. Trust requires some basic comprehension, and many citizens feel that financial institutions have become intentionally opaque.

Second, the acceleration of information flow means that trust can evaporate faster than ever before. Silicon Valley Bank's collapse in 2023 demonstrated how digital bank runs can occur at previously impossible speeds, as depositors receive information and act upon it simultaneously through social media and online banking.

Third, trust restoration occurs in a context of increasing polarization. After 2008, interpretations of the crisis quickly split along ideological lines, with some seeing it as a failure of regulation and others as a failure of government intervention. When we cannot agree on what went wrong, we cannot agree on how to fix it.

Finally, there is what economists call "moral hazard"—the problem that bailouts and interventions, while necessary to prevent systemic collapse, can undermine the very accountability needed to restore trust. When the consequences of failure are cushioned for the largest institutions, the public perceives a two-tiered system of justice and responsibility.

Yet despite these challenges, history offers examples of successful trust rebuilding. The reforms initiated by Ferdinand Pecora's investigations in the 1930s created a financial system that, for all its flaws, maintained public confidence for decades. The painful restructuring of Sweden's banking system in the early 1990s, while initially costly, laid the groundwork for a more stable financial sector that weathered later storms well.

The most effective trust rebuilding efforts share common elements: they combine meaningful accountability with forward-looking reform; they balance technical fixes with attention to cultural factors; they involve sacrifice by financial elites rather than just by the general public; and they tell a coherent story about what went wrong and how it is being fixed.

Perhaps most importantly, effective trust restoration requires time—not just for implementing reforms, but for demonstrating their effectiveness through multiple economic cycles. Trust returns gradually, tested step by step, as words align with actions and promises with outcomes.

There is wisdom in this gradual process. Financial systems built on rapidly restored but shallow trust tend to experience repeated failures. Those built on deeply earned trust, though slower to develop, prove more resilient. The societies that navigate this rebuilding process most successfully are those that resist the temptation of quick fixes and embrace the necessary but unglamorous work of institutional renewal.

In the quiet period after crisis, when emergency measures have stabilized markets but before confidence has fully returned, lies a rare opportunity—a moment when the financial system is malleable, when fundamental questions about its purpose and structure can be asked. This opportunity fades quickly as normalcy returns. The societies that use this moment wisely are those that emerge stronger from the wreckage of collapsed trust.

Like a bone that heals stronger at the point of fracture, financial systems can emerge more resilient from periods of broken trust—but only if the healing process is allowed to complete its work. Too often, we mistake the absence of acute pain for full recovery, and move on before the deeper work of rebuilding trust is finished.

Chapter 34: What We Learn, If We Learn It

In the aftermath of financial collapse, as markets stabilize and fear subsides, we face perhaps the most critical question of all: What have we learned?

The answer is both more and less than we might hope.

History suggests that we learn specific lessons quite well. After 1929, we learned about margin requirements and the dangers of excessive leverage in equity markets. After the Savings and Loan crisis of the 1980s, we learned about the perils of duration mismatches when interest rates shift dramatically. After 2008, we learned about the systemic risks of mortgage securitization and the dangers of rating complex instruments with simplistic models.

These technical lessons get codified into regulations, risk management protocols, and academic papers. They become the foundation for a new era of presumed safety. And in this narrow sense, we do learn—we rarely repeat precisely the same mistake in precisely the same way.

Yet in a deeper sense, we learn almost nothing at all.

Consider the words of economist Hyman Minsky, whose work on financial instability remained largely ignored until after his death: "Stability is destabilizing." The very success of our solutions creates the conditions for their eventual failure. We solve for the last crisis while the seeds of the next one germinate in the shadows.

After every market collapse, a curious amnesia begins to take hold. Not immediately—for a time, the pain remains fresh, the lessons vivid. But gradually, inevitably, memory fades. A new generation of financial professionals rises without the emotional imprint of disaster. New narratives emerge that explain why "this time is different." And most critically, we forget not the facts of previous crises but their feeling—that peculiar atmosphere that preceded collapse, the strange stillness in the air that we explored at the beginning of this book.

This pattern of learning and forgetting operates on multiple levels simultaneously. At the regulatory level, we see what former Federal Reserve Chairman Paul Volcker called the "regulatory dialectic"—a continuous cycle where new rules are created, market participants find ways around them, and regulators respond with further adjustments. This process creates increasingly complex systems that often address yesterday's vulnerabilities while creating tomorrow's.

At the institutional level, banks and investment firms develop sophisticated risk management systems calibrated to prevent recurrence of the last disaster. These systems work remarkably well for anticipated risks but remain blind to emerging ones. As risk expert Nassim Taleb observed, "We tend to learn the precise, not the general."

And at the individual level—perhaps most importantly—we struggle with the limitations of human psychology. We are pattern-recognition machines designed to learn from experience, yet we are also storytelling creatures who craft narratives that help us make sense of the world. When these two tendencies conflict, the story often wins.

Consider how we interpret our own financial history. After surviving a market crash, investors often develop a kind of selective memory—remembering their prescience about dangers while forgetting their participation in the excesses that preceded them. "I knew it couldn't last," they say, rewriting their personal narratives to preserve their self-image as rational actors.

This revision of memory serves a psychological purpose. It helps us maintain faith in markets and in our own judgment—both necessary for economic functioning. But it also prevents the deeper learning that might actually help us recognize the next crisis before it arrives.

What would true learning look like? It would begin with humility—an acceptance that financial markets, despite all our models and theories, remain fundamentally unpredictable in their specifics. It would include a heightened awareness of our own emotional responses to market movements, particularly the seductive pull of narratives during periods of apparent stability. And it would involve cultivating what the novelist F. Scott Fitzgerald called "the ability to hold two opposed ideas in the mind at the same time, and still retain the ability to function"—in this case, the simultaneous embrace of optimism about human progress and skepticism about our claims of financial innovation.

The philosopher George Santayana famously observed that "those who cannot remember the past are condemned to repeat it." But in financial markets, the problem isn't that we forget the past entirely—it's that we remember it selectively, learning technical lessons while forgetting emotional ones. We fix the specific mechanical failures while remaining vulnerable to the same human tendencies that created them.

This selective learning creates a peculiar rhythm to financial history. Each crisis is different in its details but familiar in its emotional contours. The Dutch who drove tulip prices to absurd heights in the 1630s would recognize something of themselves in the crypto enthusiasts of the 2020s, separated by centuries but united by the same fundamental human impulses—the desire for wealth, the fear of missing out, the comfort of collective belief, and the tendency to mistake price movements for fundamental value.

Perhaps the most important lesson, then, is meta-learning—learning how to learn from crises in ways that transcend their specific details. This means developing what might be called a "financial mindfulness"—an attentiveness to the emotional climate of markets, a skepticism toward narratives of perpetual stability, and a willingness to consider that patterns visible in the past might be repeating in new forms.

It means listening to voices at the margins, those who question consensus when consensus feels most comfortable. It means watching for the subtle signs of excess: the proliferation of financial innovations that promise returns without corresponding risk, the celebration of financial figures as cultural heroes, the widening gap between asset prices and their underlying economic fundamentals.

And perhaps most importantly, it means recognizing that financial cycles are not merely technical phenomena but deeply human ones—expressions of our collective hopes, fears, and social dynamics. The technical details change from crisis to crisis, but the human elements remain remarkably consistent.

If we truly learned this lesson, we might approach markets differently. We would still participate—still invest, still innovate, still believe in the fundamental power of markets to create wealth and distribute resources. But we would do so with a different awareness, attuned not just to the numbers but to the shifting emotional weather, the subtle changes in narrative, the quiet accumulation of pressure in the system.

We would recognize, as economist John Kenneth Galbraith put it, that "financial genius is before the fall." We would understand that the moment of greatest confidence is often the moment of greatest vulnerability. And we would approach periods of exceptional stability not with relief but with vigilance, knowing that beneath the calm surface, the forces of the next storm may already be gathering strength.

This kind of learning is difficult. It runs counter to our desire for certainty, our need to believe that we can master markets through technical expertise alone. It requires us to hold contradictions—to participate while maintaining perspective, to hope while acknowledging risk, to build while remembering that all financial structures eventually transform or collapse.

Yet this difficult learning may be our best protection. Not against specific crises—those will always come in forms we cannot precisely predict—but against the tendency to be repeatedly surprised by them. We may not be able to prevent the storm, but we can learn to recognize the stillness that precedes it, and in doing so, prepare ourselves for its arrival.

The question is not whether we will learn, but what we will learn, and whether that learning will penetrate deeply enough to matter when the winds begin to shift again.

Chapter 35: Why Hope Always Returns

In the darkness that follows financial collapse, when portfolios have been decimated and trust has evaporated, a curious phenomenon begins to emerge. It starts as a whisper, barely perceptible amid the recriminations and despair. Then slowly, almost imperceptibly at first, hope begins to return.

This return is not a matter of chance or mere optimism. It is woven into the very fabric of human existence—a biological imperative, a social necessity, and an economic inevitability.

Consider the aftermath of the 1929 crash, when the American economy lay in ruins. By 1933, unemployment had reached 25 percent. Bank failures had wiped out the savings of millions. The very concept of capitalism itself seemed to hang in the balance. Yet within this devastation, small seeds of renewal were already taking root. Families gathered around radios for Roosevelt's fireside chats. Communities organized to help their most vulnerable members. Engineers and builders continued planning bridges, dams, and buildings that would reshape the American landscape.

Hope returned not because the damage was undone—it wasn't—but because humans, by our nature, cannot exist in a permanent state of despair.

The same pattern followed the 2008 financial crisis. In the shadow of foreclosure signs and shuttered businesses, entrepreneurs were already launching ventures that would become the next generation of growth. Some of today's most transformative companies—Airbnb, Uber, Venmo—were founded during or immediately after that crisis, not despite the economic devastation but partially because of it. Disruption creates space for new possibilities.

Why does hope inevitably return after financial collapse? The answer lies in several interconnected realities about human nature and economic systems.

First, we are neurologically wired for hope. Our brains evolved to detect patterns, solve problems, and imagine better futures—capabilities that served our ancestors well as they navigated unpredictable environments. This cognitive architecture makes us remarkably resilient. Studies in neuroplasticity show that even after severe trauma, our brains gradually rewire themselves, finding new pathways forward. Financial trauma, while profound, triggers similar adaptive responses.

Second, economic systems contain self-correcting mechanisms. When assets become dramatically undervalued after a crash, they eventually attract new investment. When credit freezes, alternative financing methods emerge. When trust in institutions collapses, new institutions arise with different values and structures. These corrections aren't immediate or painless, but they are persistent.

In the years following the 2008 crisis, as traditional banks retreated from consumer lending, peer-to-peer lending platforms filled the void. As trust in financial advisors waned, automated investment services gained popularity. Each crisis reshapes rather than destroys the financial landscape.

Third, and perhaps most powerfully, humans are social creatures who find meaning in collective endeavor. After periods of financial destruction, communities often discover renewed purpose in rebuilding together. The shared experience of survival creates bonds that transcend the individualistic pursuit of wealth that often characterizes bubble periods.

Consider how the generation that lived through the Great Depression developed values of thrift, community support, and pragmatic problem-solving. Their collective response to hardship didn't just rebuild the economy—it reshaped American culture in ways that persisted for decades.

This social dimension of recovery explains why hope often appears first at local levels, in community initiatives and small businesses, before it manifests in broader economic indicators. Hope grows from the ground up, not from the top down.

Fourth, financial cycles create what economist Joseph Schumpeter called "creative destruction"—clearing away unsustainable structures to make room for innovation. The dot-com crash eliminated hundreds of poorly conceived internet businesses, but it also set the stage for more sustainable digital enterprises. The housing crisis ended irresponsible lending practices but eventually led to stronger underwriting standards and more stable property markets.

Each crisis serves as a brutal but effective editor, removing what cannot last and creating space for what might endure.

The return of hope after financial collapse isn't merely psychological comfort—it's an economic force with tangible effects. When hope begins to stir, spending gradually increases. Investment cautiously resumes. Hiring slowly expands. These behaviors, multiplied across millions of individuals and organizations, eventually generate momentum that becomes self-reinforcing.

Yet this inevitable return of hope carries its own danger. As memories of crisis fade, the lessons learned during difficult times begin to blur. The prudence born of pain gives way to renewed confidence, then exuberance, then eventually the same recklessness that preceded the previous collapse. The very recovery that heals our wounds plants the seeds of the next crisis.

This is why the most valuable form of hope is not blind optimism but what we might call "vigilant hope"—a forward-looking stance that remembers the past. It acknowledges both human resilience and human frailty. It recognizes that markets will recover, innovation will continue, and prosperity will return, but also that these positive developments carry the potential for future excess.

The investor who survived the housing crash and now cautiously re-enters the real estate market, the banker who lived through 2008 and now builds more robust risk models, the regulator who witnessed systemic failure and now designs more thoughtful safeguards—these individuals carry vigilant hope. They move forward not because they've forgotten, but because they remember.

Hope returns after financial collapse not because we are naïve, but because we are adaptive. Not because we forget, but because we reimagine. Not because the cycle has ended, but because we have found our place within it.

And in this recognition lies our greatest opportunity—not to escape the financial cycles that have characterized human exchange for centuries, but to navigate them with greater awareness, to build systems that bend but don't break, and to develop personal resilience that allows us to weather the inevitable storms while appreciating the periods of calm between them.

Hope always returns. The question is what we do with it when it arrives.

Chapter 36: How to Prepare Without Fear

There is a delicate balance to be struck between awareness and anxiety. Throughout this book, we have explored the patterns that precede financial disruption—the quiet moments before systems shift, the psychological currents that flow beneath market movements, and the narratives that both blind us to and reveal approaching reality. But knowledge without wisdom can be paralyzing. Understanding that storms come does not mean we must live in perpetual dread of the sky.

The question becomes: How do we prepare for inevitable economic shifts without surrendering to fear? How might we develop resilience without becoming cynical? Is there a middle path between naive optimism and paralyzing pessimism?

Consider the difference between anxiety and preparedness. Anxiety fixates on what might happen but offers no actionable path forward. Preparedness, by contrast, acknowledges reality and creates options. One diminishes us; the other empowers us. The distinction matters enormously for our financial, emotional, and social wellbeing.

The financial world tends toward extremes in its emotional stance. During boom times, skeptics are dismissed as pessimists who "don't get it." During busts, optimists are mocked as fools who "never saw it coming." Neither position serves us well. The vigilant middle—what we might call "pragmatic optimism"—offers a more sustainable approach.

This stance begins with acceptance of fundamental truths: markets move in cycles; human psychology drives these cycles as much as economic fundamentals; and no boom lasts forever, nor does any bust. Once we internalize these realities, we can build lives and portfolios that accommodate them without being dominated by them.

Journalist Morgan Housel captures this balance elegantly: "Optimism is usually defined as a belief that things will go well. But that's incomplete. Sensible optimism is a belief that the odds are in your favor, and over time things will balance out to a good outcome even as you endure the inevitable setbacks."

This is not merely philosophical positioning. It translates to concrete approaches for navigating uncertain economic waters.

The most resilient financial strategies share common elements that protect against downturns without sacrificing participation in growth. They embody preparation without fear.

First is the principle of appropriate liquidity. Cash is often derided during bull markets as "dead money" that produces no return. Yet maintaining a cushion of liquid assets—typically three to six months of essential expenses—provides both practical protection and psychological comfort during turbulent times. This isn't money hidden under mattresses out of paranoia; it's a deliberate shock absorber that allows you to weather job losses or unexpected expenses without forced liquidation of long-term investments at precisely the wrong moment.

Second is the practice of diversification across uncorrelated assets. This isn't simply about owning stocks and bonds, but about understanding how different assets respond to various economic conditions. Real diversification means owning assets that don't all move in the same direction during crisis—a lesson painfully relearned during each market collapse when previously uncorrelated assets suddenly begin moving in lockstep.

A thoughtful investor might consider: equities for growth during expansions; high-quality bonds for income and relative stability during contractions; perhaps some allocation to real assets as inflation protection; and potentially alternative investments with different risk profiles. The specific allocation matters less than the underlying principle—not placing all hopes on a single economic scenario.

Third is the recognition of personal risk tolerance. The mathematically "optimal" portfolio is irrelevant if it causes such anxiety that you abandon it at the worst possible moment. As the behavioral economist Daniel Kahneman noted, "Regret is the emotion we experience when we can easily imagine having made a different decision that would have led to a better outcome." The most sophisticated investment strategy fails if regret drives you to sell at the bottom or buy at the top.

Financial resilience extends beyond asset allocation. It encompasses career flexibility, skill development, and relationship cultivation—what we might call "human capital diversification."

Consider how the pandemic revealed the vulnerability of seemingly stable industries and the resilience of others. Those who had developed transferable skills, maintained professional networks, and cultivated multiple income streams generally weathered the disruption better than specialists with rigid career paths.

This doesn't mean everyone should become a "slash worker" with multiple part-time gigs. Rather, it suggests developing an adaptive mindset that views skills as portable assets and relationships as sources of opportunity and support during transitions. The consultant who also teaches, the engineer who writes code for multiple industries, the manager who understands both operations and finance—these hybrid professionals create options for themselves that pure specialists may lack.

Perhaps the most challenging aspect of preparation is maintaining awareness without succumbing to anxiety. The human mind struggles with sustained vigilance—we either grow complacent or become hypervigilant, neither of which serves us well.

Financial history offers a solution: ritual examination rather than constant monitoring. Just as physicians recommend annual check-ups rather than daily self-diagnosis, financial health benefits from structured review rather than obsessive checking.

This might mean quarterly portfolio reviews, annual reassessment of emergency funds, or periodic "stress tests" of your financial situation against hypothetical scenarios. These structured check-ins create space for thoughtful evaluation without the emotional drain of constant worry.

Equally important is information hygiene. During both booms and busts, financial media amplifies extreme voices. The most pessimistic forecasters gain audiences during downturns; the most wildly optimistic attract followers during upswings. Neither extreme typically offers useful guidance for long-term decision-making.

Instead, cultivate information sources that provide context rather than emotion, history rather than hysteria, and principles rather than predictions. Seek voices that acknowledge complexity and uncertainty rather than promising certainty in an inherently uncertain domain.

Throughout financial history, certain individuals and institutions have demonstrated remarkable resilience across multiple cycles. Their approaches offer valuable lessons.

The endowments of institutions like Yale and Harvard, guided by investors like David Swensen and Jack Meyer, survived the 2008 financial crisis despite significant losses because they maintained liquidity buffers that prevented forced selling. Their long-term orientation allowed them to use the crisis as an opportunity rather than a catastrophe.

Family offices of multi-generational wealth typically prioritize capital preservation over maximum returns, understanding that avoiding ruin matters more than maximizing gain. This "survival first" mentality—focusing on avoiding catastrophic loss rather than achieving the highest possible return—has protected wealth across centuries of financial turbulence.

Even at the individual level, those who navigate multiple financial crises successfully tend to share certain traits: they maintain reasonable debt levels, build multiple income streams, invest regularly through all market conditions, and perhaps most importantly, they separate their sense of self-worth from their net worth.

While individual preparation matters, financial resilience ultimately requires collective action as well. The most prepared individual remains vulnerable in a society without adequate safety nets, regulatory frameworks, or crisis response mechanisms.

This suggests that true preparation includes civic engagement—supporting policies that create systemic resilience rather than fragility. This isn't about politics in the partisan sense, but about recognizing that financial systems are human creations that can be designed for either stability or instability.

The financial regulations implemented after the Great Depression created decades of relative financial stability until their gradual dismantling preceded new crises. Similarly, the social insurance programs developed during that era—unemployment insurance, Social Security, and later Medicare—created resilience that helped prevent economic downturns from becoming humanitarian disasters.

Engaging with these systems—understanding how they work, supporting their improvement, and participating in their governance—represents a form of preparation that extends beyond personal finance into civic responsibility.

There is a curious paradox in preparation: the better prepared you are, the less likely you are to need your preparations. This creates a cognitive trap where preparation seems unnecessary precisely when it's most effective.

Consider the Y2K computer bug that threatened to disrupt global systems at the turn of the millennium. Massive preparation efforts largely prevented serious problems, leading many to conclude the threat had been overhyped. The success of the preparation made the preparation seem unnecessary in retrospect.

Similarly, those who build financial buffers rarely need to use them to their full extent precisely because having those buffers changes their decision-making. The emergency fund reduces financial stress, which improves job performance, which reduces the likelihood of job loss.

The diversified portfolio reduces anxiety during market drops, which reduces panic selling, which improves long-term returns.

This paradox helps explain why preparation often seems irrational during calm periods. The benefits remain largely invisible—manifesting as disasters that don't happen and crises that don't materialize.

There is a profound freedom that comes with thoughtful preparation. Rather than constraining us, it liberates us from both denial and dread.

Those who prepare without fear can engage more fully with present opportunities, knowing they have created resilience against future disruptions. They can take calculated risks from a position of security rather than desperation. They can view market cycles with curiosity rather than terror.

This freedom extends beyond financial decisions into life choices. The person with adequate financial buffers can pursue meaningful work rather than merely lucrative work. They can prioritize relationships over accumulation. They can make decisions based on values rather than fears.

In this way, preparation becomes not merely a defensive posture against potential storms, but a foundation for a more intentional life—one where financial considerations inform but don't dominate our choices.

As we stand in this moment—perhaps in the calm before another storm, perhaps not—we have the opportunity to choose our stance. We can ignore the patterns of history out of willful optimism. We can obsess over them out of paralyzing pessimism. Or we can acknowledge them with clear eyes and prepare with calm hearts, knowing that whatever comes, we have done what we reasonably can to create resilience.

The storms will come, as they always have. But with preparation without fear, we need not be defined by them. We can instead be defined by how we weather them, how we help others through them, and how we rebuild after them—with greater wisdom and more durable structures, both financial and social.

In the end, that may be the most valuable preparation of all.

Chapter 37: The Storm Is Not the End

There is something almost sacred in the aftermath of a storm. The air clears with a crystalline quality. Sounds carry differently. Colors appear more vivid against the washed landscape. And in this clarity, we begin to see things as they truly are.

Financial storms follow similar patterns. After the panic subsides, after the blame has been assigned and the wreckage assessed, there comes a moment of extraordinary lucidity. The financial world, briefly stripped of pretense and excessive complexity, reveals itself in simpler terms. What remains standing is what was truly valuable all along.

I have walked through the quiet streets of Manhattan in October 2008, when the financial district seemed to hold its breath. I've seen the empty tech campuses of Silicon Valley after the dot-com collapse, abandoned foosball tables gathering dust in lobbies once filled with the sound of champagne corks. I've studied the photographs of Wall Street in 1929, men in fedoras standing in uncertain clusters, their world suddenly unrecognizable. And in each case, what followed was not an ending, but a transformation.

The storm is never the end. It is merely a forceful transition.

Consider the Great Depression, which brought unimaginable suffering but also created the conditions for the most equitable economic expansion in American history. The regulatory frameworks established in its wake—the Securities and Exchange Commission, the Federal Deposit Insurance Corporation, the separation of commercial and investment banking—created decades of financial stability that allowed for the greatest middle-class prosperity the world had ever seen.

The 2008 financial crisis, for all its pain, accelerated a reevaluation of what constitutes meaningful work, sparked a renewed interest in financial literacy, and forced a generation to question assumptions about debt, homeownership, and the promise of endless asset appreciation. From its ashes rose new approaches to sharing resources, from the growth of the sharing economy to community-supported agriculture, from renewed interest in walkable neighborhoods to experiments with universal basic income.

Even the collapse of the dot-com bubble, which seemed catastrophic at the time, cleared away unsustainable business models and excessive speculation, allowing capital and talent to flow toward the technologies that would actually transform our world: social networks, smartphones, cloud computing, and the digital infrastructure we now take for granted.

In each case, what appeared to be destruction was also creation. What felt like an ending was also a beginning.

This is not to minimize the very real suffering that accompanies financial collapse. Jobs lost, homes foreclosed, retirement dreams deferred or destroyed—these are not merely statistics but profound human tragedies. The storm brings real damage that cannot be dismissed with facile optimism. Some wounds never fully heal.

But to see the storm only as destruction is to miss half of its nature. Economic crises force reckonings that comfort never would. They compel us to question assumptions, to dismantle systems that have outlived their usefulness, to imagine alternatives that prosperity made unnecessary. They create spaces for voices previously unheard and ideas previously dismissed.

The most important question is not whether another storm will come—it will—but what we will build in its wake.

Will we merely reconstruct the same vulnerable structures that collapsed before? Or will we use the moment of clarity that follows upheaval to envision something more resilient, more equitable, more aligned with our deeper values? Will we remember what the storm revealed about what truly matters?

During financial panics, we discover that relationships matter more than portfolios. That skills endure when credentials lose their luster.

That community provides security when institutions falter. That meaning and purpose sustain us when material comforts cannot.

These insights arrive with painful clarity during crisis. The challenge is to preserve them during recovery.

History suggests this is our most difficult task. As markets recover and confidence returns, we tend to rebuild the very systems that failed us, perhaps with modest reforms around the edges. The fundamental questions raised during crisis—about the purpose of an economy, about what constitutes real value, about the proper relationship between finance and human flourishing—fade as prosperity returns.

Yet each generation has the opportunity to learn more deeply than the last. To carry forward not just technical lessons about leverage ratios and counterparty risk, but philosophical insights about what an economy is for and who it should serve.

The storm is not the end. It is an invitation to begin again, with greater wisdom.

When the winds have passed and the rain has stopped, when the financial markets have found their new equilibrium and the economy has begun its slow recovery, we face a choice. We can rush to rebuild what was lost, or we can pause in that moment of extraordinary clarity to ask what should be built instead.

The answer to that question—more than any technical regulation or policy reform—will determine whether the next period of calm truly represents progress, or merely the quiet before another storm.

www.ingramcontent.com/pod-product-compliance
Lightning Source LLC
LaVergne TN
LVHW090403210926
848480LV00002B/431